Helena
Unwavering Courage
By
Sylvia Melvin

Joann,
I hope you enjoy
my grandmother's story.
Sincerely,
Sylvia Melvin

This is a true story. None of the names have been changed and all of the events happened as related to the author by members of the family.

This book is dedicated to my grandmother, Helena Maude Matthews. Her courage, faith and devotion to her five children was an inspiration to succeeding generations.

Acknowledgments

The author may plant the seed of a manuscript, but experience has taught me before it becomes a finished book there are special folks along the way who've contributed to its development. Helena: Unwavering Courage is no exception. A heartfelt thank you to:

My husband Al- Your support and patience went above and beyond.

Myra Shofner- Your exceptional editing skills motivated me to get the job done.

Tommie Lyn Blackburn- Your assistance in preparing a manuscript for online publishing was essential.

Emily Podlogar- Your determination to find the correct computer program resulted in a great looking cover.

Margie Baldwin- Your assistance in converting files was so important.

Bill Walton- Your willingness to supply me with photos of the Kawigamog was truly appreciated.

David Noran- Your expert knowledge of antique automobiles resulted in finding me the exact auto wagon drawing.

The Panhandle Writers Group- Your support was amazing.

Thank you, one and all.

Sylvia

Chapter One

Helena Matthews woke from a restless night's sleep with a queasy feeling in her stomach. At first she thought it was the familiar morning sickness she'd experienced at the first signs of her fifth pregnancy, but she was well into her ninth month. This was different. Intermittent jittery waves of emotion washed over her leaving a residue of physical and emotional anxiety. Her legs slid slowly over to her husband's side of the bed searching for the familiar touch of his body. Empty. The coolness of the sheets sent little chills through her limbs and she remembered James speaking to her sometime after sunrise.

"Don't get up, Helena. You must have been uncomfortable last night. Tossed and turned a good bit and I'm sure you're tired. I'm going down to the lake to check on my boat. If the children hear me they'll want to come ride in the auto wagon. I shouldn't be long. Tell them we'll take a ride up to Bain's farm this afternoon."

Drowsily, Helena responded, "Uh-huh. Be careful, dear."

The feather-like brush of James's mustache on her lips was the last thing Helena remembered as she slipped back into an uneasy slumber.

By eight o'clock the familiar sounds of children jumping out of bed, energized and ready to tackle a new day, brought Helena to her feet. Breakfast was first on her agenda and as she stirred the oatmeal and prepared the coffee to perk, she kept an ear out for the return of the auto wagon. *Hmm, James should have come home by now. He never goes without his breakfast.*

Helena wiped the dripping water from the last of the meal's bowls, glancing up at the kitchen clock every few minutes. *Where was he?* Trying to put her concern aside, Helena finished baking a strawberry pie and was thinking of what to prepare for her family's lunch when she heard a knock at the door.

"Ruby, go see who's at the door, please. I need to finish slicing this ham." Out of the corner of her eye she glimpsed her daughter scurrying toward the front entrance. As Helena cleaned the grease off the knife's blade and carefully placed it back in its rack, familiar voices grew louder as they followed Ruby back into the kitchen.

The smile on Helena's face faded and without warning another round of the uneasy feeling she'd felt earlier gripped her stomach as her eyes took in Reverend Malcolm and two other men, their faces downcast and shoulders slumped. Sensing that something was amiss, Helena felt her legs weaken and her mouth became so dry she could barely tell Ruby, "Go play with your brothers and sisters." Turning to her visitors, Helena went on, "Good morning. I'm afraid James isn't here. Took his auto wagon down to the lake but I expect him home anytime. Should be getting hungry about now; he didn't stop for breakfast this morning."

Each of the men, with their hats in their hands, looked at Helena nervously. One shuffled from foot to foot,

2

another cleared his throat a couple of times as though he wanted to say something but finally the Reverend broke the uneasy silence. "Helena," he pulled out a chair and suggested, "you need to sit down. I have some bad news to tell you."

Helena's hand grasped her chest. "Something has happened to one of the children?"

"No, it's not the children."

She looked into Reverend Malcolm's tear filled eyes. Her body quivered as a cold numbness took possession of her senses and she struggled to say, "J...J...James?"

The Reverend nodded as he took her hand and it was Jake Brown's turn to explain. "Some of us fellers was headin' down the hill to work on a log boom when we looked back and seen him comin'. Figured he was going to check on his boat. He was no sooner past us when one of those big rubber tires hit a rock stickin' out of the grass and over she went. We all yelled, 'Jump, Jim, jump.' But it was too late."

Helena's face froze in fear. One part of her wanted to yell, "Stop! No more!" but another part begged for details.

Jake hesitated, unsure of what to do.

"Please," Helena sobbed, "go on; tell me everything."

Jake produced a red-checked handkerchief from one of his overall pockets and handed it to Helena before continuing, "We hauled his body out from under that darn wagon and someone told the Stephens kid to go fetch the Doc. But Jim was gone; crushed his skull. I'm so sorry, ma'am."

Helena stared at her messenger in disbelief then collapsed in convulsive sobs. After a few moments, gasping for breath, she managed to say, "The children—I've got to tell them. And my family."

3

"That's already been taken care of Helena." The Reverend continued, "One of the Simms boys volunteered to ride over to Restoule a half hour ago. My wife should be here soon with women from the church to help out 'til your mother gets here. Listen, I can stay and break the news to Edith and Ruby if you like. Billy may have trouble understanding. Harry's too young."

Helena's response was swift. "No, I want to tell them—before they hear it from their friends. But if you could stay, it might make it easier."

"Of course."

Putting their hats back on, Jake and his son volunteered, "We'll send them over; saw them playing with the Stephen's girls. Anything we can do to help, you let us know."

"Thank you, Jake." The tears of the wounded woman continued to flow.

***

Exhausted from the events of the day, but determined to keep the children's usual bedtime routine, Helena's feet felt like bricks as she trudged up the stairs to tuck her offspring under their sheets. One peek into Billy and Harry's room showed her that both boys were asleep. The sound of whimpering from the room across the hall caught Helena's attention. She went into the girls' room and sat down on the edge of the bed.

"Mama," Edith reached for her mother's hand and began stroking it. "I'm so sad; now when I wake up Papa won't be sitting at the kitchen table with you drinking his coffee. He'll never be there. He used to tug at my braids and tease me about my freckles. Told me a cow sneezed bran in my face."

4

"I miss the stories he told us at bedtime," recalled Ruby. "Remember the one about chasing the bear? Was that true, Mama?"

"One never knew with your father, girls. Seems he wasn't afraid of anything. Wouldn't surprise me."

"I don't ever want to see that ugly auto wagon again." Edith's resolute expression prompted Helena to explain.

"You won't have to, dear; Grandpa Campbell tells me men from the Masonic Lodge are coming to the funeral and will take it to North Bay. That's over seventy miles away. Listen to me, girls. It's o.k. to cry. I've cried all day and I expect I will all night. And to tell you the truth, I'm a little angry, too. Not at you children. It wasn't your fault, but maybe a little at your father for buying that contraption."

"Mrs. Malcolm told us at church that if someone hurts you God expects you to forgive, Mama." Edith continued, "Do you think you can forgive Papa? You still love him, don't you?"

Helena reached out to gather her girls in her arms. "Always and forever; without him, I wouldn't have you precious children." Tucking her daughters under the quilt, Helena gave each a kiss then walked into her empty room. Tonight no husband would lay by her side; tonight she was alone with her faith. *Lord, help me; please help me.*

Chapter Two

Helena lifted trembling hands to part the delicate lace curtains. She pressed her face against the bedroom window, and watched through eyes stinging with tears as the mourners in the somber, black funeral procession accompanied her husband's body to the village cemetery that would harbor his remains.

The fifteen men, all wearing the apron of the Masonic Lodge, walked in order of rank ahead of the horse drawn wagon. One of their brothers, John James Matthews, a thirty-second degree Mason, had met his fate and they were paying him the tribute he deserved. Behind the wagon came the familiar faces of friends and neighbors; men, uncomfortable in hot dark suits, women dressed in long dresses and carrying parasols, and children in their Sunday best. They endured the July noonday heat as they paid their last respects to James Matthews, devoted father, entrepreneur and a man who never met a stranger. He was part of this remote northern Ontario community and they felt the void of his passing.

Helena longed to leave the room in which she was confined, run after the wagon and touch the pine box — a last physical contact with James. She watched as their friends moved out of sight leaving behind lingering particles of dust in the air, stirred up from the horse's hooves and the creaking wagon wheels.

Helena turned from the window and before she took another breath, a contraction sent fiery spasms into the small of her back. She winced and fell back into the pillows on her feather bed, unable to tell which hurt worse -- natural pain of childbirth or the emotional torment of losing a loved one. The first one had been nine months in preparation, the other was instant. She rolled her rotund body from side to side in an effort to squelch the discomfort but the effort intensified her distress. Grief, accented with pain, forced her to cry out, "James is gone, Mama. Gone. What am I going to do?"

Her mother's soothing fingers pushed back the shining, straight black hair that fell across Helena's forehead. It was the familiar touch she'd known since childhood when the softness of her mother's skin had calmed her fears. Today's adversity strengthened that bond of love again.

"Dear, you'll always have a part of him with you." Her mother fought for composure. "Remember the children. Any hour now, you'll have a new baby. Another reminder of James's love." Helena's mother squeezed her daughter's hand, "I know your heart is crushed but you're not alone. Your father and I, along with your brothers and sisters, will help you. That's what families do. You think for one minute I could ever neglect my precious grandchildren? Lean on your faith, Helena. It will not let you down."

"Oh, Mama, you've always been strong, but you had to be. You were one of the first women to come up from the south and settle here. James was like you --so capable; so confident. I felt protected and secure. He was my mighty oak; I'm just a wispy willow."

"Have you forgotten," Her mother brushed a stray strand of hair from Helena's forehead, "that the willow's strength lies in its roots. It might get tossed about, but, it still bends. And when the storm is over, those branches are still there. You'll be strong too; I know you. Try to rest now. Your baby's going to need all your help."

Calmed by her mother's presence, Helena settled quietly into an uncomfortable rest as the hours ticked on, minute by minute, second by second. Three hours later, the contractions became more frequent, more intense and Helena sobbed in anguish until finally, with the assistance of a mid-wife, her mother placed a fragile baby girl in her arms.

"Annie", Helena whispered, as she looked into the face of the little girl who had breathed her first breath of life two days after her father took his last. Her lips pressed against her daughter's forehead and she breathed a fervent prayer, "Lord, how will I ever raise five children alone? Please help me."

And with that Helena Maude Matthews fell into an exhausted sleep.

John James Matthews

The funeral procession, led by the Masonic Order, filed past the white Matthews homestead where Helena, in labor, watched as her husband, James, is taken to the village cemetery.

The Masonic Order and friends walked to the cemetery.

Chapter Three

For the next three days, Helena remembered little except the constant pressure on her breast as Annie sought nourishment. Her sleep was deep and for most of the day her body craved its healing restoration while her mind kept slipping into the past, back to the homestead at Restoule, another small village twenty miles from her present home, where she was raised with her brothers and sisters. The log house with its large two-story structure had been built to serve two purposes-- one, to house a family, and the other, to accommodate men going into the lumber camps at Loring. The half-way house was filled with hearty laughter, activity, and the anticipation of meeting new faces.

Andrew Hill, a widower from Sault St. Marie, Ontario, walked through those doors one day. He stole Helena's young heart and they became engaged. Helena thrashed about in her bed as this painful memory flashed by. Death had stolen her first love, too, when fourteen days before their wedding, her fiancé died of typhoid fever leaving her crushed. She held on to fragments of faith until self-pity turned to fortitude and a sense of maturity.

13

Not long afterward, James, foreman for the Ontario Lumber Company in Loring, began taking refuge at the half-way house on a regular basis and noticed Helena's strength of character. As the pain of losing Andrew became easier to bear, Helena at age twenty-nine, quiet and serene, found herself anticipating the visits made by this man with the penetrating soft, green eyes, neatly trimmed mustache and strong facial features that bore a determined look.

"Marry me Helena," James persisted. "I want to be the one to make you smile again. I can give you a good life. We've just turned a new century and northern Ontario is the place to be. There are so many opportunities with the demand for our virgin stands of hemlock and pine. The loggers can't cut the trees fast enough and the sawmills are turning out lumber and shipping it south every day. I see the future, my dear, and I want us to be part of it."

Helena gave her heart to James and six months later, July 10, 1905, they were married. She stepped up into their carriage, her stomach fluttering with the excitement of beginning a new life with her husband in a fledgling village where she knew no one. Waving good-bye to her family, she tried to keep her composure but the glistening moisture on her cheeks caught James's attention and he reached over, squeezed her hand and said, "I believe the Good Book puts it this way: 'And a man shall leave father and mother, and shall cleave to his wife: and the twain shall be one flesh.' Right?"

Helena took out a snow-white linen handkerchief, wiped her cheeks clean and smiled at her husband. "How could I forget; I'll miss them but you're the most important part of my life now." James returned her smile and squeezed her hand again. Helena continued, "I can't wait to make our home as comforting as the one I was raised in. The walls of that house have heard it all- laughter, cries of excitement, sobbing. Just the everyday chatter of my brothers and sisters was enough to raise the roof."

"That's the part I want, Helena. Children. I know you're going to be a great mother. Being the eldest, my guess is you've had plenty of experience helping your mama and there should be no doubt in your mind I'll be a good provider."

"I've never doubted that for a second; what with all your ideas and visions for our future you keep my head spinning."

"It's a wonderful time to be alive, Helena. The turn of the century has brought so many new inventions and the opportunities are endless. But it takes determination and the courage to take risks. Are you with me?"

Eyeing the gold band on her left hand, Helena replied, "'Til death do us part."

Lulled by the motion of the bouncing buggy and the exhaustion of the wedding festivities, Helena leaned her head against her husband's shoulder and soon fell asleep. The warmth of the sun caressed her skin adding to the sheer pleasure of the ride. After a while she sensed that they were no longer moving. She forced her lids open. The journey was over; she was home.

"James," Helena gazed at her house and gasped, "You mean this is ours? I never dreamed you'd build a home like this. Two stories. A bow window extending from the parlor and a covered full length porch!"

"Now you know why I insisted you wait until we were married before you saw it. It's my wedding gift to the woman I love."

"Thank you." She threw her arms about his neck and showered him with kisses. "I've known from the beginning there was something that set you apart from other men."

Lifting his wife down from the carriage, James instructed, "Walk up to the door, Helena. There's one more surprise."

Helena skipped up the front steps and as she reached the last one her eye caught the glint of ruby red, brilliant blue and sparkling yellow panes of stained glass surrounding the oak door.

"Well?" urged her husband as she tried to find the appropriate words.

"It's ...so elegant, James. Where did you ever find the glass around here?"

"Had it shipped from Toronto. Came up by train to the depot in Trout Creek, then Matt Stevens brought it in on his wagon. I could imagine a box full of nothing but shattered glass after traveling over thirty miles of ruts and bumps."

"It came over two-hundred miles!"

"Why be satisfied with the ordinary, my love?" Helena's delight amused James. "Reach beyond. Be different. We walk through life only once and I intend to live it to the fullest—to give it my all. It's going to be an exciting ride, Helena. Hang on. I hope you're ready."

The Matthews homestead housed Helena and her five children

Chapter Four

Life with James the first year of marriage was everything he told her to expect. Never having met a stranger, often James would arrive home at mealtime with one or two new acquaintances eager to sample Helena's cooking. After a number of these unexpected guests appeared on their doorstep, Helena caught on and peeled two or three extra potatoes to throw into the pot. Stimulating conversation over a second cup of coffee often centered around politics or some entrepreneurial scheme. At the same time, James, always eager to get ahead, was working seven days a week.

Helena was not reluctant to voice her displeasure.

"Ever since you started this farm implement business, James, Sunday's become just another work day to you. I sit in church by myself. No husband by my side. Everyone stares at me and asks questions. Where's James today? Busy again? Can't you rest one day a week?"

"Helena, you know logging timber is a winter job and many of our men turn to farming in the spring." James was not to be persuaded to change his ways. "They depend on me to supply the tools. Having plows and scythes here in the village saves them time. Time is money to them. Can't you see it's my way of helping out?"

Exasperated, Helena gave a long sigh, turned and almost collided with the local reverend as he poked his head in the shed.

"Couldn't help overhearing as I walked up, folks. Must admit I agree with Helena. Shouldn't be working on Sunday, James. I notice you've been doing that a lot lately. Why don't you stop unpacking those crates and come with me?"

James walked up to Reverend Malcolm, looked him in the eye and said, "Tell you what Reverend, I'll make you a deal; I'll come to church today if you'll show up here Monday morning and help me set up these implements."

"The Lord willing I'll be here by sun up, James."

With a twinkle in his eye, James replied, "I'll be counting on you both, Reverend."

Helena smiled from ear to ear as she walked into the ten o'clock service on her husband's arm.

***

The highlight of the first year of marriage came when James announced he was taking Helena on a train ride to Toronto two-hundred miles away. For a week she was transported into another world. Instead of horses, they rode on trolley cars, instead of cooking, she ate food prepared and served by others and even their room was cleaned by a maid. James spared no expense when his wife gasped at the sight of a fashionable hat in a millenary shop.

"No, James," she protested. "Where would I wear it in Loring?"

"Around the house if you choose too, my dear. Some day I intend to take you places you have never been and you'll need a fancy hat."

18

The seven days spent exploring the city came to an end and the couple once again boarded the north bound train. They made one stop in Orillia, James's hometown, as a recent letter from his family indicated that his brother was ill and wished to see him. Although pleased to meet the Matthews family, Helena felt uneasy around the sick man. His constant coughing and pale color indicated a serious disease. Her suspicion was confirmed a month later; James's brother was laid to rest—cause of death— tuberculosis.

For the next several months, at the least sign of a cold or a cough, Helena worried that James might have contacted the contagious virus. In his usual way, he scoffed at her concern.

"Stop worrying. I'm healthy and strong."

"But there's a weakness in your family. Your mother told me."

"That doesn't mean T.B. is going to take me, Helena. I refuse to live in fear."

Finally, after many laundry washings, Helena stopped looking for signs of blood in his handkerchiefs, a major indicator of the terrible disease that ravaged the body and killed so many.

Helena knew no other man with such a passion for life. She recalled the day James came bounding into the kitchen carrying a newspaper and exclaiming, "Look, Helena! Here is the airplane I saw at the Toronto Exhibition where men called Barnstormers were taking folks up for a ride."

"And I suppose you were itching to go, too, James Matthews."

"I paid my money and was all set when it started thunderin' and lightning; they cancelled the flight. Sure was disappointed; can't think of anything more exciting than flying."

Helena gave a sigh and looked upward. "Thank you for sending the storm, Lord. Maybe He was trying to tell you something, James. If men were supposed to fly they'd sprout wings."

"Don't be surprised if one day I fly one of those machines, Helena. You know I love a challenge." Those words continued to echo in Helena's ears days after her husband's death. *Yes, but this time you paid the supreme price.*

The knot in Helena's stomach grew tighter and she tossed from one side of the bed to the other as she recalled the day that monstrous machine arrived in Loring. It was the talk of the town for weeks. Anticipation grew and Helena tired of answering the same question everywhere she went.

"When's James bringing that contraption home?" coupled with the hushed whispers of those who clung to the old ways. "Dang fool, if you ask me. Waste of money. This part of the country ain't ready for somethin' that belongs in the city. Thought James had more sense."

Word spread quickly the day James arrived with his new purchase. Curious townsfolk crowded around the eighteen foot mass of wood, steel and glass, asking question after question. Could it really travel twenty miles an hour? What made the headlights glow in the dark? Why did a large chain extend from the underside of the wagon to the engine in front? How was it able to back up? And the one unasked question on everyone's mind was what could possibly motivate a man to invest in such an uncommon piece of machinery?

Helena had asked herself that question a hundred times during the several weeks she and James discussed the advisability of such a move. It was the dominant topic of conversation in the Matthews' household between husband and wife.

"But you've never driven anything but a team of horses, James."

"They'll teach me everything I need to know, dear. It can't be that difficult. Other men are doing it, aren't they?"

"Yes, but it must be different in the city; they aren't driving on wagon roads with deep ruts, mud and boulders," persisted Helena. "Besides, how will we ever afford such an expense?"

"That's the beauty of it, Helena," his voice grew in excitement. "The machine will pay for itself. Let me explain. How do we get our goods and supplies?"

"They're brought up from the south by train to the station at Trout Creek. Somebody has to pick them up by horse and wagon," replied Helena.

"And how long does it take to travel thirty-eight miles? A day and a half if the weather is good," continued James as he answered his own question. "I can cut that time in half. Not only will I be able to deliver to the general merchants in the village, but the increasing number of lumbering operations on the lakes will welcome this service. I'll transport their supplies from the motorized wagon into my inboard boat on Wilson Lake and continue my delivery by water. Think of it, Helena. I'd be the first in these parts to operate a gas driven wagon."

"What if folks think we're being uppity?" She didn't want to dampen her husband's enthusiasm, but always the realist, Helena continued her end of the debate. "You know, I've heard talk behind our backs. The Captain certainly won't like it."

"I don't care if Captain Kelsey likes it or not." James bristled. "You know he and I don't always see eye to eye, especially since it's been rumored I refused to sponsor him into the Lodge. We can't let what others think influence a golden opportunity, Helena."

Helena accepted the futility of arguing further. International Harvester had just sold a 1913 Auto Wagon.

International Harvester Auto Wagon

Chapter Five

If Helena was less than zealous about the motorized wagon, the children in the village made up for her, especially when they heard the huge rubber horn that protruded from the driver's side.

"Please, Mr. Matthews," they begged, "take us for a ride."

Bodies bounced and frolicked in the back of the wagon while shouts of joy and screams of delight echoed over the bumpy pathways. The wind tousled their hair as the vehicle gained speed. Only one child, James' own three-year-old Billy, clung to the fence and refused any part of the horseless contraption. He eyed it with suspicion and ran when he heard the rattle of its engine. Even his mother shied away from her husband's offer of a ride.

"Come, now, Helena," coaxed James, "it's perfectly safe. You know I'd never put you in danger; especially with the baby coming. Please let me take you and the children up to Bain's farm tomorrow."

'We'll see what tomorrow brings, James. No promises."

Chapter Six

Two weeks after the funeral, the soft light from the kerosene lamp flickered on the pages of Helena's Bible which lay in her lap, opened to the book of Ecclesiastes. Each night she returned to the third chapter reading it over and over as the words put life into perspective for her.

"There is a time for everything, and a season for every activity under heaven: a time to be born and a time to die, a time to plant and a time to uproot, a time to kill and a time to heal...

"God," she whispered, "I know you are in ultimate control of everything; and there's nothing I can do to change that. It's just that I feel so weak. Helpless. Afraid. You know I'm left with fatherless children. Lord, I need your strength to meet this challenge." Helena paused to dab at a renegade tear that threatened to spill onto her Bible. " Please help me be the strong woman James would want me to be."

***

Like the bud of a tree in spring, slowly responding to the warmth of the sun, Helena began to emerge into reality for longer periods of time each day. At first, all she wanted to do was retreat from her daily routine; pull the covers around her like a cocoon and hibernate. But Annie's cries of hunger demanded she get out of bed and tend to her infant daughter. Besides, she loved the way her baby cooed and wrapped her fingers around her thumb as the milk that flowed from her breast satisfied and filled Annie's tiny stomach.

The urge to participate in familiar activities grew stronger and one afternoon she got up from the table, marched outside and picked up the hoe, exclaiming to her mother, "I won't lose the garden, too. Look how the weeds are taking over the squash, and the cucumbers. Why, at this rate, I won't have nary a one to make pickles and you know how J...James likes..." Her voice trailed to a whisper as she realized her mistake but immediately came back with, "the boys eat my dills."

As the summer greenery silently changed to crimson, yellow, and orange then tumbled to the earth to offer protection against the forthcoming cold, sterile blanket of snow, Helena knew it was time to stand alone.

"We have to talk, Mama," she began one evening after the children were bathed and tucked in for the night.

"From the tone of your voice, dear, this sounds serious. What is it?"

"I can't continue leaning on you; if I'm ever going to stand on my own it has to be in these early months. I have to do it now. If I don't, I'll become more and more dependent on your strength." Helena's voice trembled but she was determined. "With winter coming on, Father needs you at the house in Restoule. You know travelers are soon going to demand your attention. After all," she smiled, "you're the best cook in northern Ontario."

Grandma Campbell's face reddened as she scoffed, "Oh, now, I've plenty of competition, but there's some truth in what you're saying. It takes several pairs of hands to keep up with all the work. But, dear, are you sure you're ready?"

Helena reached for her mother's hands and squeezed them as she continued, "The Lord has blessed me with a wonderful family and you're only twenty miles away. If I need you one of the young lads in the village can ride over and fetch you. In fact, I'll speak to one tomorrow about taking you back. How can I ever thank you enough for all you've done?"

"There's nothing more important than family," Grandma Campbell responded. "That was His plan from the beginning and it will never change. But, Helena, I have to confess; I'm going to miss the children."

Helena, fighting back her own stinging tears, reached and wiped away the tear which found its way out of a grandmother's glistening eye and meandered down a soft, warm cheek.

28

Chapter Seven

Sparks from the burning wood in the fireplace exploded and crackled as an evening stillness replaced the noisy activity heard earlier in the day. Billy and Ruby sat cross-legged on the parlor floor engaged in a challenging game of checkers. Edith, pretending to be the teacher, insisted on reading aloud a passage from one of her school books, and Harry, exhausted from all his boyish antics, was curled up on the rug asleep, storing up energy for the morning. Annie, lay nestled in her mother's arms.

The chiming of the grandfather clock reminded the children that no matter how they begged for more time, it would do them no good. Their father had set the rule and Helena intended to keep it enforced. After kissing each one good-night, she returned to the parlor and picked up her knitting . One look at the diminishing ball of wool and she realized she needed more. *Now where did I put that new skein I bought?* Helena pondered a moment and then she remembered. *In the drawer in the sideboard.* As she reached inside for the wool, a familiar scent moistened her eyes. Pipe tobacco. Lying in a wooden box were three of

29

James's favorite pipes. Staring at the wooden bowels, her fingers caressed the finely carved stems and the opening where his lips had drawn in the pungent smoke. *When did you last smoke from them, James?*

The loneliness Helena felt at the moment was reminiscent of those nights her husband had left her with the children while he traveled to the nickel mines in Sudbury selling gold chains, watches, and valuable gemstones to the miners in the camps. It was another of his business ventures that had proven to be profitable. During the fall season, Goldsmiths Jewelry in Toronto, supplied James with three to five thousand dollars worth of merchandise and he earned a percentage of each sale. At first, accessibility to the miners was a problem since miles and miles of dense forest separated him from his customers. But, with his usual ingenuity, James found the solution. He traveled over the frozen terrain with a dogsled and a team of six brawling canines. This year the well traveled route would lie undisturbed holding a secret never to be revealed. Hidden somewhere between Loring and the Sudbury mines, a good sixty miles, James stashed a portion of his goods.

Helena searched her brain until her head ached for any clues that might unveil the hiding place. She distinctly remembered sitting at the kitchen table taking inventory with her husband after his last trip. He handed her a package of three dozen gold chains and instructed, "Lena, these are solid gold. Put them in a safe place."

Examining the chains, she replied, "No, James, you're mistaken. Look, here on the box it says 'gold-filled'. These are not solid gold."

For a moment James' facial muscles tensed but instantly he relaxed as he recalled, "You're right. I hid the others on the trail until I go back."

"But why? You've never done that before? How will you ever find the exact spot out there in all that wilderness?"

"Not to worry, my dear. I've traveled that area so often I know it like it was my own back yard. The chains are well protected. I buried them beneath the branches of a spruce that hides the entrance to a cave-like crevice."

"I still don't understand why you didn't bring them home." Her rebuke urged her husband to explain.

"It was a warm day close to breakup and as I came to the river to cross over, I saw that the ice had thinned considerably since the week before. I didn't want to take a chance that the dogs might break through and I'd lose everything on the sled; so I hid the box of jewelry. I know exactly where it is and I'll get it on my first trip back." James patted Helena's hands. "Now, are you relieved?"

"James, you never told me you'd put your life at risk crossing that river. It's not the gold chains I care about."

"Life is to be lived; one shouldn't be afraid of it. Where is your faith, woman?"

"Oh, James," Helena murmured, as she recalled their conversation, her lips scarcely moving, "there will be no return trip or retrieved gold chains. But there will always be an emptiness in my heart."

The rhythmic clicking of her knitting needles brought her back to reality. Immediate family needs must take priority. Right now, Edith and Ruby needed long wool stockings to wear under their bloomers as they braved the below zero temperatures on their daily walk to the one-room, log school house. And she must knit mittens and toques for them, too—extras to keep on hand for the times the mates were lost or displaced as so often happened. Knitting was a skill of necessity and there was always a project in the making.

"It won't be long," mused Helena, "when Edith's little fingers will be mature enough to handle the needles. She does so favor her father—a quick mind that seems to see beyond her age."

31

An abrupt knock at the door startled Helena. It was followed by another.

"Who on earth is out on such a freezing night?" The knocking startled her. "It must be twenty below zero. And what could they possibly want of me?" She dropped her knitting into the basket, drawing her shawl closer in anticipation of the blast of frigid air that comes from an open door.

"Mrs. Matthews," a familiar voice called, "May I come in?"

"Why Mr. Currie, of course; you'll catch your death standing out there. What can I do for you?" She opened the door to one of the local farmers.

"I apologize for the lateness of the call, Ma'am, but the animals had to be fed and a few other chores done before I could leave. Not too many idle moments on a farm, ya know."

"I understand. You have a good sized place, too, don't you?"

"It's comin' along nicely, Ma'am. In fact, that's kind of why I'm here."

"Oh?"

"You see," Mr. Currie took a deep breath, shuffled his feet and went on, "last summer just before James was killed, I bought a plough from him. He gave me six months to come up with the money and I figured you'd be needin' it 'bout now."

A tender smile on Helena's lips spoke the truth. Many times since James' death, the same story had repeated itself. Business transactions she knew nothing about suddenly came to light. Honest folks paid their debts.

"Thank you," Helena's voice broke as she wiped her eyes. "It's people like you who've given me the faith and hope I need to raise my five children."

"You lost a mighty good man. It's the least we can do. Sure will miss that farm machinery business he had. It

32

was right handy for a lot of us farmers. Saved time not having to wait for something to be shipped from down south—not to mention the trip out to the train depot to pick it up. Well, I've gone on long enough." He reached in his pocket and pulled out a well-worn leather pouch. "Here's the money. Twenty-five dollars. I don't have no bill of sale statin' the price. You know how James was—your word was good enough for him."

"I trust you, Mr. Currie. You wouldn't be here if I couldn't," replied Helena. "Thank you so kindly."

"You're more'n welcome, Ma'am. Good-night and God bless you and the little ones."

"Oh, He does. I'm convinced of that. My best to your family."

The click of the latch shut out the cold while the warmth of the past few minutes lingered. She faced a shaken future, financially, but she was very certain about one thing. God had not left her alone. Once again, His spirit had shown up on her doorstep through a local farmer. Where would she see Him again?

Chapter Eight

The sound of clanging anvils and pounding hammers awakened Helena as surely as if she'd set her alarm clock. She climbed out of bed, slipped on her housecoat, and walked to the window. Across the fence, loading an armful of split oak logs into a wheelbarrow was Matt Stephens, a tall, muscular village blacksmith. An important craftsman in the community, he lived with his wife, Mary, and eleven children in a three story, box-like structure next door to the Matthews family. A board fence with a few missing planks separated the two. The boundary division was unnecessary as perfect harmony existed between them.

In a separate building back of the house, Matt kept the glowing forge burning night and day as steel melted and was molded into the shape of horse-shoes so crucial to the animal's hooves. Not only were his services vital, but so were those of his deaf and dumb brother Anthony, affectionately known in the community as 'The Dummy'.

"Mama," Billy asked one morning as he sat at the table eating his oatmeal, "why do we have to use our hands

35

to talk to Len's uncle? And why do people call him Dummy? I don't think he's dumb at all."

"You're right, Billy. Len's uncle is one of the smartest men I know. Folks don't call him Dummy to be mean; it's just that he can't hear our voices or talk to us. He was born deaf and we have to make him understand with sign language. But God gave Anthony a very special talent. You've seen how he can take a piece of plain wood and use his hands to carve beautiful things. In fact, he made the pine box your father is resting in." Helena stopped before her voice became shaky.

Unaware of his mother's emotion, Billy's face lit up with excitement. "Mama, do you think he'd make me a gun?"

"A gun!" Helena lay down the knife she'd been using to cut into a loaf of bread, reached across the table and pointed her finger into her son's chest. "Billy Matthews, whatever gave you such an idea?"

"I heard Len's big brother say that soon everyone is going to have to get a gun cause there's a big war going on. He told Mr. Forsythe over at the store that he's gettin' one."

"And just where's he going to get a gun?"

"He's joinin' the army. Says he's gonna fight the Krauts. Wish I could too, then I'd have a real gun. Mama, who are the Krauts? Are they comin' here?"

Helena put her hands on her eldest son's shoulders, looking into eyes that exposed naïve understanding of war. "You know from your school work that the country of Germany is across the ocean. A very long way from Canada. Most of the people are good and decent but sometimes leaders get greedy and want more power, more land and they do terrible things to get them. They have to be stopped so men from other countries are risking their lives to put an end to this war."

Helena pulled Billy into the softness of her chest, silently praying a word of thanks that in all his innocence he was not old enough to leave home and join the ranks of men who were laying down carpenter tools, horse's reins, shovels, axes, implements of whatever trade they boasted to pick up rifles and bayonets. For months, rumors of war with Germany had circulated via the newspapers. Even Loring, a sparsely populated village, was not immune to the stories. At first, it seemed as though it was just that—a terrible story being acted out on some foreign European stage far from home. But with each friend, neighbor or relative that joined the cast, the reality of war became a fact of life. For an instant, a chilling thought played with Helena's imagination. *What would James have done? He'd never been one to back down from anything; instead of losing him from a crushed skull, I could have easily been a war widow.*

"Oh, Lord," she silently prayed, "bring these men home to their women. War is so futile; and life is so short at the best of times."

With the world in chaos, shortages and inflation became an increasing problem. No one was spared—rich or poor. Helena watched her meager savings dwindle with each purchase: one-hundred pounds of sugar cost thirty dollars; one dozen eggs sold for one dollar and twenty-five cents. The list seemed endless. So did the war.

More than once during 1917, Mary Stephens came to Helena with a heavy heart, her plump little body panting in fear. "Helena, you're so strong. I just don't know if I could bear it if Bill doesn't come home. I pray faithfully to our Blessed Virgin Mary to keep watch over him. Now, to make matters worse, Cleo is wanting to join his brother."

Helena gently placed her arm around Mary's shoulder and seeing her moistened cheeks she pulled a spotless white handkerchief from the neck of her housedress and wiped away the wetness.

37

"Mary, you're doing the best a mother can do for her son. I know from experience that prayers are heard. Yours will be, too. And as for Cleo, you know how young men like to talk big."

"You're probably right," Mary sighed. "I don't mean to burden you with my worries. Land sakes, you've got enough of your own."

"Mary Stephens," Helena was firm. "What would I've done these past four years if you hadn't listened patiently to my grief? I owe you more than words can say. Take heart, Mary, the Bible tells us there is a time for war and a time for peace."

The waning months in 1918 brought hope of victory and fear of defeat as the weekly newspapers reported on battles either won or lost. The announcement everyone in Loring prayed for came from an unlikely source. Thomas Smith, one of the local farmers reported having gone to the train depot in Trout Creek to send a telegram and was heading out the door when all of a sudden the telegraph machine started tapping out the message, "War is over. Peace at last. Armistice Day, November 11, 1918."

Passengers waiting to board the train threw their arms around each other shouting, "It's over! We won! Thank God! No more war." Thomas wasted no time in spreading the good news to everyone he met along the thirty-eight mile ride back home. By the next day, the ringing of the church bell drew men, women and children together for a time of rejoicing and prayer.

Helena looked at the bereaved faces of those who'd lost a father or a son. Her heart felt their pain; she understood all to well the grief they were going through. But then, she saw the relief and joy of those who once again would feel the arms of their beloved around them.

"Thank you, Lord," she whispered, "Peace at last."

Chapter Nine

"Hey, it's my turn," shouted an angry voice. "Let me slide."

"You've already broken yours, Ken. Sue's next in line. Down you go, Sue," commanded Edith.

Helena turned the latch on the front gate puzzled at the sound of hostility. Although no one was visible, she recognized the robust enthusiasm of Billy and Harry. And was that Annie crying?

Helena quickened her step. As she turned the front door knob, an explosion rattled the glass panel. Swinging the door wide, she was greeted by a thud, thud, thud. Instantly, a streak of blond curls landed at her feet. For a moment, Helena could not utter a word; shock numbed her speech as she stared at the scene before her. Like a hill of swarming ants, children shoved past each other and climbed the steep stairway that ran from the second floor to the first. Each child was carrying the remnants of a window screen.

"Mama, watch us slide," squealed Harry as he positioned himself on the top step. With a push from his sister Ruby, he was at the bottom in a flash grinning from ear to ear.

"Stop! Stop!" Helena's voice cut through the children's jabber like a scythe-clean and sharp. One look at her furrowed brows and tightened jaw brought immediate silence. "What on earth are you children doing sliding down the stairway on these window screens?" Disbelief knotted her stomach as she picked up a wooden frame. Silver mesh dangled from its once secure bindings. Ruined. A quick survey told the truth; not one could be salvaged. Eight useless screens.

Helena was beyond anger. Her leaden legs collapsed into the first chair she saw as she buried her face in her hands. Sobs erupted from within releasing a floodgate of tears. She fought to control her irregular breathing. After a few moments, she raised her head to see that the neighborhood children had left and her own children, faces somber and remorseful surrounded her.

"We're sorry, Mama." whispered Edith.

"It was Billy's idea to pretend we were sledding," hastened Harry.

Little Annie, not accustomed to her mother being angry, clung to Helena's skirt, while Ruby inquired, "Are you alright, Mama?"

Wiping her eyes, Helena explained, "Yes, I'm alright but I'm disappointed in your behavior. Edith, I thought I could trust you to care for your brothers and sisters while I was at the church." Helena picked up a piece of the carnage. "Do you realize how long I saved to buy those screens? Now that summer is coming, we'll have to use the old ones that are rusted and rotted. How did you find them?"

Billy confessed. " Yesterday I saw Mr. Thompson bring you a big box. Remember, he told you our chicken feed went to Kelsey's store. I wanted to know what was inside so I looked until I found the box in the cellar. I only wanted to try it once but then all the other kids wanted one, too." His voice quivered with remorse.

Helena reached for her son, bringing him into the softness of her bosom.

"I'm proud of you for telling me the truth, Billy. Guess you remembered the lesson from church yesterday, after all. Well, we'll just have to make do with the old screens this summer and every time a mosquito bites, it'll remind you of your actions today. That will be your punishment, won't it?"

Four heads bobbed up and down at the thought of getting off with nothing but a mosquito bite. "Yes, Mama." Only Annie, too young to comprehend the seriousness of their escapade, remained silent.

The confrontation with the children was over. The boys scampered out the door with Billy announcing, "We're going down to the creek to catch frogs, Mama." Edith picked up Annie and headed toward the kitchen with Ruby close behind. Helena watched each one disappear hopeful that though chastened, they were wiser.

Chapter Ten

Each time Helena looked out a window, she visualized the tattered, shiny new screens that lay in a heap inside the storage shed. Thrifty to the penny, she intended to at least salvage the wooden frames to be used for kindling.

The loss of the screens was bad enough but to know that the bag of chicken feed went to Kelsey's General Store was more than Helena could tolerate. She carefully checked the Eaton catalogue order form. Yes, the company marked off eight screens, one pair of rubber boots, three yards of broadcloth, six skeins of wool and one bag of chicken feed. Not only did she have written proof, but an eye witness. Bert Thompson, whom the village depended upon to pick up and haul supplies the thirty-eight miles from the train depot, put the bag of feed on the sleigh himself. A small hole located near the bottom of the sack set it apart from the others.

"Your chicken feed went to Kelsey's store, Helena. I'm sorry it was taken off the sleigh before I noticed. Just tell Captain Kelsey it's the one with the hole in it. This is the last trip I'll be making for a while now that spring breakup is here."

"I appreciate your concern, Bert. I'll take the matter up with him. You can be sure of that."

Helena's breath quickened and the nerves in her stomach tightened at the thought of confronting the Captain. Not once since James's death had he expressed one breath of sympathy to her. Of course, she knew James and the Captain had never seen eye to eye. Something about the man bothered her husband to the core. James never discussed the specifics of his feelings with Helena, but rumor had it that James refused to sponsor Captain Kelsey into the Masons.

Helena knew she could not let another day go by; she had to take a stand today. Placing her worn, felt hat over her black, braided knot of hair, Helena straightened her skirt, held her head high and with determination in each step climbed the hill to Kelsey's General Store. Once inside, her legs began to shake and her mouth felt dry and parched. For an instant, she battled with the thought of retreat but taking a deep breath she looked around for the Captain. Her eyes combed the interior of the store. He was nowhere in sight. A couple of clerks were waiting on customers so Helena walked up to the counter and inquired, "May I speak to the Captain, please."

A tall man, wearing a clerk's apron, studied her momentarily then asked, "Mrs. Matthews, right?"

"Yes. I won't take but a minute of his time."

"He's in the back shed checking on a new shipment of supplies. I'll tell him you're here."

Helena acknowledged her appreciation with a brief nod. As she waited, her nostrils twitched at the pungent odors of goods on display: leather harnesses, tobacco, cheese, peppermint candy, and spices. Scanning the interior, she saw the shelves overflowing with yard goods of various colors and textures. *No doubt Mrs. Kelsey with her sense of style and fashion is responsible for this display*. Helena sighed. How long had it been since she'd sewn herself a new dress? Her eyes shifted to sacks of flour and sugar, bins of nails, tools, lanterns, coal oil lamps and other household necessities. There was even a section displaying ladies bonnets, gloves, boots and parasols.

In time, Captain Kelsey appeared, his face red and stern. He moved toward Helena and began impatiently drumming his fingers on the counter. "What is it, Mrs. Matthews? I have customers waiting." Clean, unweathered hands nervously adjusted the ties on his shopkeeper's apron.

Helena took a deep breath and stood tall. "I have reason to suspect, sir, that a bag of chicken feed I ordered from Eaton's catalogue came here by mistake." She looked the arrogant little man straight in the eye.

The corners of his well-groomed mustache began to twitch. "Are you accusing me of stealing, Madam?"

"No, sir, I'm simply inquiring. Do you have an extra bag of feed? According to Bert Thompson, when he put it on the sleigh he noticed a small hole in the sack. Could you check your supply please?"

A red glow crept up the side of the Captain's neck, his breathing quickened and he straightened his shoulders as his voice rose in indignation.

"Indeed, I will not. Why, I distinctly recall taking inventory myself the day Bert delivered supplies. I received only what I ordered."

Piercing eyes sent little chills through Helena and she trembled as she continued, "Perhaps your helper, Mr. Rose…"

"Mr. Rose was ill and not at work that day."

Refusing to lower herself to the point of argument, Helena straightened her shoulders, looked into the man's reddening face and announced, "Captain, I shall survive the loss of one bag of chicken feed. After all, I've lost much

45

more than that, haven't I?" Without giving him a chance to rebut, Helena turned and, with head held high marched out of the store. If he thought she was going to beg, he was sadly mistaken.

That afternoon, one of the village children delivered a note to Helena.

Mrs. Matthews,

After over-hearing your conversation with Captain Kelsey this morning, I must tell you in good conscience that yesterday someone bought a bag of chicken feed with a hole in the bottom of the sack. I'd appreciate your discretion as my present employment would be in jeopardy should the Captain know I told you. William Rose

Helena folded the evidence and said a silent prayer of thanks that at least one honest man worked at Kelsey's General Store.

***

Even though the village was small, the residents of Loring encouraged competition among general merchants. And it was stiff competition. Located directly across the road from the Matthews homestead, stood the grandest building in town. It towered two stories high with a balcony over-looking a front porch. The façade, crafted by the Dummy with his creative genius, resembled the white lace edging found on a fine linen tablecloth. Attached to the right wall, the local post-office handled the incoming and out-going mail. Sitting by itself, a freight shed overflowed with carpenter's tools. The owner, Ed Forsythe, knew the needs of the community and served them well. From early morning until long after the sun sank into the horizon, folks came and went. It was a local social center where neighbor met neighbor and comments, advice and everyday chit-chat was exchanged.

Helena smiled as she walked up the steps onto the porch where some men were engaged in conversation.

"Better get that hay in this week, boys," announced an old timer to a couple of young farmers loading up their wagons with supplies. "Gonna' rain; I can feel it in my joints. Happens every time."

"Ah, you can't put no stock in your old bones, George," argued his checker-playing opponent. "Keep your mind on this game before I beat you for a second time."

"Looks like there's going to be a Federal election called for sometime this fall," reported a young clerk after reading the headlines in the recent newspaper. "My vote goes to that Mackenzie King fellow. Sounds as though he's all for helping us poor folks instead of lining his pockets like most of them government guys do. And listen to this," his voice raised in indignation, "some woman by the name of Agnes Macphail wants to run for a seat in parliament! Can you believe that? It'll never happen. What are women thinking these days?"

"Now just a minute, young man," Mrs. Forsythe chimed in, "women have always been the backbone of this country. Why shouldn't she have a say in how its run? We're a lot stronger than you think. Just look at Helena Matthews over there raising those lively young'uns on her own."

"Speaking of the Matthews' boys," the preacher continued, "they put on quite a show for us folks a couple nights ago. We were sittin' around on the porch here chewin' the fat and all of a sudden we hear this hootin' and hollerin' coming from one of their upstairs windows. There they were, naked as jaybirds, in the liveliest pillow fight you ever saw! Why we were so caught up in it we'd even taken up sides. Feathers flew in all directions. That is until their mother, downstairs in the sitting room, realized what caught the crowd's attention. Before another feather floated to the floor, Helena hightailed up the stairs and into the boy's bedroom and pulled down the shade. The show was over for the spectators on the outside, but by the sounds coming from inside, Helena did not spare the rod. Those boys reaped the reward of the seeds they'd sown."

"Boys will be boys," laughed Ed Forsythe as he swept the dust off the porch steps. "That Billy's a feisty one; couldn't be more like his daddy. Hard little worker, too. Heard him tell his sisters yesterday that Mary Smith, over at the boarding house told him she'd pay him a nickel if he'd pile a stack of wood for her. Apparently he did the job 'cause he came in here, five pennies in hand, and left with a bag full of sweets. Course Grandma was behind the counter and the kids know she'll fill it to the brim; she's got a soft spot for those young'uns. Last I saw, all five of them were sitting under the haw tree munchin' licorice and gum drops." Ed sighed and shook his head from side to side. "Wouldn't surprise me if Helena had to get the castor oil out for a stomach ache or two last evening."

"All I can say," volunteered one of the local ladies, "is if you want to catch up on the town's news, just come sit on Forsythe's porch a spell. Better than any newspaper. Guaranteed. Straight from the horse's mouth."

Chapter Eleven

Helena woke to the singing of robins. Each day the chorus grew louder and she welcomed the sound. *I love to hear one of the first signs of spring. It's so reassuring; a promise from God that everything starts out new again.*

To the early 19th century residents of northern Ontario, spring break-up was more than a natural phenomenon; it was deliverance from the bondage of blinding blizzards, ice-locked lakes, below zero temperatures and social isolation.

Waking from its frozen slumber, the village of Loring stirred with new life. For the women, spring meant thorough housecleaning, no corner was left untouched. Warm, fresh breezes blew through open windows chasing out stubborn, stale lingering winter odors, while freshly washed blankets clung to sagging clotheslines. Windows scrubbed with kerosene and water sparkled in the welcome sunlight. Like animals shedding their winter coats, woolen mittens, hats and scarves were cheerfully deposited in the bottom of cedar chests. A sense of freedom was in the air and no one realized it more than the children. Pent-up energy exploded into all sorts of activities after the cloistered months of short days and long nights.

While Helena and the other women in Loring were busy with housekeeping duties, the anticipated annual chore of making maple syrup began. For approximately two to three weeks, Mother Nature sent revitalizing sap from the roots of the maple tree up to each branch. However, not all of this nectar would reach its destination as during maple sugar time, one could drill a hole in the bark of the tree, drive a spile into the hole, attach a bucket and let the sap drip continuously until it overflowed. Helena boiled the sap until all the water evaporated and only the sweet aroma and golden glow of maple syrup remained. A few trees supplied her need but for some families, like the Stephens, making maple syrup was a much larger operation.

About a half mile from town stood a groove of hundreds of maple trees. Here, gallons of sap were gathered and stored in huge wooden barrels until it was time to boil off another batch. Iron kettles, blackened with time and smoke hung over red-hot flames, their contents bubbling and churning sometimes far into the night until at last the perfect texture was reached. Finally, after dripping through a cotton strainer, the precious liquid was sealed in mason jars and left to cool. It took not only forty gallons of sap to make one gallon of syrup, but also, uncounted hours of toil and patience. But oh, the rewards were worth it; velvety syrup, mouth-watering taffy, and savory sugar were treats not to be found in any confectionary.

There was no place on earth as far as the children were concerned. With all the trees and bushes, it was an ideal place to play Hide-and-Seek. Imaginations ran rampant as young saplings skillfully transformed into bows and arrows for the tribe of Indian maidens and warriors who chased each other in their world of fantasy, affectionately known to them as Windigo.

"O.K.," instructed Ken Forsythe to a small gang of village youngsters, "I got my eyes closed and I'm counting to ten; you'd better run and hide cause if you don't and I see you, I get to tag you with my arrow and you have to join my tribe."

"Yeah, but don't forget, if someone sneaks up behind and tags you, you're not 'It" anymore," reminded Billy.

"Just try it," boasted the Chief of his tribe, "I bet I'll tag everyone of you."

"What do you want to bet?"

Ken rammed his right hand into a pocket of his overalls and produced a colored sphere. "This here marble."

"It's a bet; start countin'."

For the next two hours, the games continued with hootin' and hollerin' bouncing off the maple trees and dissipating in the afternoon breeze.

Not only did this particular sugar bush appeal to the innocent fun and frolic of the younger children, but it also harbored some teenage mischief as well. Since Prohibition was now the law of the land, there was always a market for home brew. Mary's son, Sid, a devilish lad of seventeen, cleverly used the guise of distilling sap as a cover-up for making whiskey. That is until Billy Matthews foiled his plans.

It was during one of those fierce battles of make-believe when this stealthy young buck cautiously slithering from tree to tree in an attempt to evade his pursuers, found himself several hundred yards away from the normal circle of activity. Panting and thirsty, he headed for a large barrel sitting under the branches of a maple tree. It was common practice for the children to drink the cool sap stored in such containers so it came as quite a surprise to Billy when he lifted the lid to scoop up a handful of liquid a terrible smell assaulted his tender nostrils. With a child's curiosity, he looked closer. This was no barrel of sap. Determined to learn more, he picked up a long stick, rammed it into the barrel and started stirring the foaming, mysterious mixture. It had a yellowish-brown tinge to the color and as the stick delved further, a thicker mixture swirled to the top and then settled slowly back down to the bottom.

"Hmm," thought Billy. "This looks like mash." His nose wrinkled as he inhaled another whiff of a familiar ingredient he'd often smelled in his mother's own kitchen —yeast. One thing was certain; he wanted no part of this concoction. Slowly slipping the lid back in its original position, the truth of what he'd witnessed started to dawn on him. Could this be the home brew he'd overheard a couple of men talk about one evening over at Forsythe's store? Now he remembered as his eye caught a burlap bag lying on the ground. They were buying grain and one of them was joking that this was one bag the cows would not see.

Sensing that he was in unwelcome territory, Billy picked up his bow and high-tailed it out of there. Home was on his mind now and besides, the sun was beginning to set. From the sound of silence around him, it was clear that the other children left their "Windigo" world and were well on their way to a waiting supper.

Helena counted heads as the children came through the door, washed their hands at the sink, and found their place at the supper table. *One, two, three, four. Where was the fifth?*

"Edith, where's Billy? Didn't he come home with you?"

A chorus of voices tried to answer.

Helena tapped the metal ladle on the table. "One at a time; Edith?"

"He ran away, Mama. Into the woods cause he didn't want Ken to catch him."

52

Harry couldn't contain himself. "Maybe a bear got him!" One look from his mother was all Harry needed to know that this was no joking matter.

"We called his name," Ruby said, "but he didn't answer. We thought he came home another way."

"Bow your heads for the blessing" instructed Helena, her mind on her missing child. "Thank you, Father, for our food."

Ruby's small voice chimed in, "And please send Billy home soon."

While the children ate, Helena walked outside and looked up and down the gravel road. The only form she saw silhouetted against a darkening sky was that of a stray goat munching grass along a split-rail fence.

By the time she returned to the kitchen, the girls were cleaning up the table and Harry was draining the last drop of milk from his glass. Then she heard it-the squeak of the back screen door. In walked her son, a look of guilt on his dust smudged face.

Relief, tinged with anger, caused her to blurt, "Billy Matthews, why didn't you come home with your brother and sisters?"

Hoping to ward off any due punishment, Billy's voice rose with excitement, "Mama, I have to tell you something really important."

Helena placed a bowl of steaming stew before the child and instructed, "Wash your hands and come tell me. I was getting so worried; both you and Harry know I don't like you out in the bush after dark."

"But that's where I found it, Mama." Billy's voice suddenly became almost a whisper. "It's a secret between you and me. Promise."

Helena leaned closer. "You'll have to tell me what you're talking about, child."

"Somebody's making home brew up on the Stephen's sugar bush."

A gasp fell from Helena's lips. Billy had her undivided attention.

"How do you know? You've never seen an ounce of that vile liquid in your life."

"I did today, Mama. And it looked and smelled terrible!"

"Billy, you know it's against the law to drink and make whiskey. Mr. Stephens is a good Christian man and he'd never do such a thing. Now, you start from the beginning and tell me exactly what you saw in the maple sugar bush today."

By the time Billy recounted the events of the day, Helena knew he was right. The barrel was full of the makings for homemade whiskey. A heavy weight descended upon Helena's spirit and she didn't sleep well. The Stephen's family were her dearest friends and neighbors. She couldn't accuse them of a wrong-doing. Perhaps, though, someone else was squatting on their property. If this were the case, then Matt needed to know. Her chaotic mind kept racing from one scenario to another and her restless body tossed and turned until the bedsheets were no longer anchored to the mattress.

Drained from lack of sleep, Helena went through the motions of preparing breakfast in a preoccupied state. Oblivious to the blackening toast, Ruby was the one to bring her mother back to reality.

"Mama, I smell something burning! It's the bread. Quick, lift it off the stove. Are you o.k., Mama? You don't look good."

Shaking her head to clear the mind fog, Helena picked up the wire toaster and assured her daughter, "I'm fine dear, just a little tired this morning. I didn't sleep well last night. Not to worry. Now go get your brothers and sisters to come to the table while I cut more bread."

Helena made the decision over her second cup of coffee. She'd find Mary and tell her Billy's story right after she cleaned up the kitchen. This stocky, little woman was not hard to locate. As was the usual routine, almost every day she hung out a load of laundry. With a family the size of hers, one did not even question it.

"Helena, good morning," she called over the fence as the last of the sheets she'd been hanging flapped in the wind. "Is everything alright dear? You look a little tired."

"Can you spare me a few minutes, Mary? We have to talk."

"Of course." She left the clothes line and closed the gap between them. "What is it?"

With a deep breath, Helena reached through the missing board in the fence and took Mary's hand. She repeated the tale Billy told her and waited for her friend's response. Slowly, with eyes closed, Mary shook her head back and forth as she made the sign of the cross. A look of enlightenment came across her face and she said, "So, that's what's been going on."

"You know something about this?" Helena questioned.

"It all falls into place, now, Helena. Just two days ago, Flo complained to me as she was doing the baking that the sugar bin seemed emptier than it should be. I just got a new bag not long ago. I reminded her that we do feed a large family. She agreed with me but insisted that we've never used that much sugar in such a short time. The raisins were in short supply, too. It seemed she went to put some in the cookies and only about a cupful was in the canister. I immediately thought that Sue and Len were treating their friends again. Remember the day I caught them with their fists right full?"

Mary continued as another piece of the puzzle was solved.

"And even this morning when I went to set my bread, only two cakes of yeast were on the shelf. Someone has been helping themselves to my pantry, and I think I know who it is."

"Tell me," urged Helena.

"Sidney," Mary replied without doubt. "His daddy caught him drinking with some other fellas last Saturday night. So I guess he's decided to make his own. Well, we'll just see about that." A devious smile crossed Mary's chubby face as she explained, "My Sid is going to discover that the old expression 'too many cooks spoil the broth' is true. I believe his recipe needs one more ingredient. In the back of my cupboard is a five pound box of Epsom salts. Just wait t'il they start mixin' with the rest of that brew! My son's inards are never going to be the same! I'll be making a trip up to the sugar bush with Billy as my guide if you don't mind, Helena."

Laughter erupted until the bodies of the two women shook like jelly as they imagined the results.

If Sid Stephens wondered why his mother, who seldom found time to visit the woods, decided to pay a call that particular afternoon, he found out when he pulled the cover off that hidden barrel. One thing was certain; maple syrup was the only liquid that left that sugar bush bottled in mason jars.

From the left, Edith,
Harry,
and Annie
play in the sugarbush

Chapter Twelve

A sense of excitement ran like an electrical current throughout the village that first day of July as young and old looked forward to celebrating Canada's birthday, at a giant picnic held in an open field less than a mile from town. Days before the festivities, the aroma of tarts, cookies, pies, and cakes permeated every kitchen up and down the country lanes while mothers' eyes kept a keen surveillance on those who might be tempted to indulge before the proper time and place.

The children, especially the boys, ran to get the cows, ran to do their chores, ran with each other, all in preparation for the special races each was confident of winning. Even the older men toned up their aim around the horseshoe pits and, no doubt, the heavens heard prayer after prayer pleading for sunshine to brighten the day.

"Are we ready?" Helena asked as she surveyed five eager faces, each scrubbed and shining with anticipation.

"Yes, Mama, let's go," begged Harry dancing and prancing on one foot and then the other. "The Forsythe kids are probably there by now and I know I can beat Ken in the races this year."

"You might beat Ken," challenged Billy, "but you can't beat me."

There was enough smugness in her eldest son's tone to prompt Helena to stop any sibling rivalry before the frolic began.

"Listen to me, you two, there'll be no fighting or arguing today. Is that clear? It's going to be a great day; we're celebrating our nation's birthday and we should be proud."

Two heads bobbed up and down in agreement.

"Then let's get a move on," continued Harry.

Since the picnic was within walking distance, Helena and the children fell in with the parade of neighbors who chose to walk rather than hitch up a wagon and ride. Besides, it was a good opportunity to chat with folks not seen for a while. One such gentleman spotted Helena immediately and within seconds was at her side.

"Mrs. Matthews, let me carry your basket; you've got quite a load."

Unprepared for any male attention, Helena almost stumbled as her head turned to see William Rose reach for her burden.

"Oh, Mr. Rose, how kind of you to offer. It seems the boys have tired of my slow pace and are well ahead of me."

"Please, call me William."

"And I'm Helena."

"What a lovely name."

William's compliment sent an unexpected blush to Helena's cheeks and she directed her gaze back to the moving crowd. "I hope the boys aren't being too pushy."

"Looks like they're raising some dust all right. But then I'm sure they're eager to take part in the races."

"They've talked of nothing else all week."

"Mama," interrupted Edith as she gave William a disdainful look, "I could've carried the basket."

"You already have the quilt, dear. I appreciate Mr. Rose's help."

Edith walked on in an uneasy silence, giving William an occasional sideways glance as the conversation between him and her mother continued.

"I'm surprised Captain Kelsey allowed you to come to the picnic, William."

"The store is closed today. I've a feeling Mrs. Kelsey convinced her husband that all his customers would be spending their money at the picnic. I understand she's one of the organizers."

Since the conversation was centered on William's employer, Helena cautiously continued, "I haven't been in Kelsey's General Store in some months so I haven't had the opportunity to thank you for the note you sent concerning the chicken feed. I appreciate your honesty."

"It was the least I could do. I'm sure you've quite enough on your mind with five children to care for. I felt you deserved to know the truth. I must admit, it saddens me to think the Captain took advantage of the situation."

"Well, I survived and so did the chickens. They're just a little leaner that's all."

Edith turned in time to see a smile cross the faces of both adults. Her shoulders slumped and her face flushed crimson. *Why was her mother even talking to this man – much less smiling at him?*

Soon, shouts of greeting and warm embraces welcomed young and old as townsfolk left their burdens and cares behind them to indulge in mouth-watering food and heart warming fellowship. Each family brought a favorite spread to relax on making one area of the field look like a gigantic colored quilt. Another section was a hive of perpetual motion with bodies of all dimensions competing in baseball, horseshoes, races, and games.

"Over here, Helena," came the voice of a friend. "I've saved you a spot."

Edging her way through the maze, Helena motioned the others to follow. Much to Edith's annoyance, William was close behind.

"Josephine, how good to see you," Both women embraced then Helena stepped back and inquired, "Have you met Mr. Rose, er, I mean William? He works for the Captain." Turning toward William, she continued, "Josephine is my closest friend."

William sat the basket on the ground and extended his hand. "Pleased to meet you, Ma'am."

"Likewise," replied Josephine eyeing this gentleman with obvious curiosity. "How nice of Helena to invite you."

"She didn't invite him," volunteered Edith who stood protectively by her mother's side still clenching the quilt.

Surprised by her daughter's irritation, Helena took the quilt and spread it out close to Josephine's. "William kindly offered to carry our basket. Won't you join us, William?"

Before he could form the words, Edith plopped right in the middle of the quilt, spreading her arms in one direction and her legs in another, leaving little room for an intruder. Giving the child no satisfaction, he simply stated, "I'd be delighted; this grass looks quite comfortable."

"Nonsense, you'll share our spread. Edith, why aren't you with the other girls? Up on your feet this instant. Ruby has already found Sue."

"Me too?" a soft voice begged. Annie, coming out from behind Helena's skirt had no intention of missing any fun.

"Yes, little one, your big sister will take you, too. Won't you, Edith?"

Knowing better than to refuse, Edith reluctantly got up, grabbed Annie's hand and pulled her alongside toward the other children.

"What's troubling her?" asked Josephine. "She's never been one to pout. We have a grand time when she and Ruby come down to the farm."

"You've got me. She can be one independent child when she fancies. I'm sure whatever is bothering her will pass before the day is through."

Helena looked forward to July the first as eagerly as anyone, for as much as she loved her children, she did miss adult conversation. It seemed there wasn't enough time in a day to complete the required daily household tasks and socialize, too. Here, she not only shared in the amiable atmosphere of the women, but this year, enjoyed the attention of a male friend as well. And very attentive he was; even to the point of cheering Harry on to possible victory as the child tried for the seventh time to defeat his peers in the races.

Bending down to help this determined six-year-old tie his boot, William noticed Harry's dusty legs and a bright red scrape on his knee. "Looks like you took a tumble. Sure you're up to this race?"

"Got to; want my Mama to be proud." A shy smile creased the corners of his mouth and he caught Helena's eye.

"You can do it, son; run as fast as a you can! Cheered Helena from the sidelines as Harry moved into his starting position.

"Ready, set, go!" yelled a man in a felt hat chewing on a plug of tobacco.

A cloud of dust filtered through the crowd as folks strained to see the fastest runner. Cheers of victory welcomed the winner. But not for Harry. Once again, he failed to meet his expectations.

"Maybe next year, Harry," consoled William as the child's frustration rose to tears. "Say, I bet some ice-cream would bring a smile to that face."

Instantly, Harry's spirits soared. "Sure would. See," he beamed.

"Helena, may I treat the family? No picnic is complete without freshly made ice-cream."

"I don't want any," stated Edith. She turned and lost herself in the crowd before Helena could stop her.

"Please excuse her rudeness, William. I'll speak to her later."

"No apologies needed. The rest of us will enjoy what she missed. Are we ready, kids?"

Their deafening response left no doubt that the remaining family members intended to savor this man's generosity.

Chapter Thirteen

The late afternoon sun inched its way down through the sky and hovered over the horizon casting gaunt shadows along the edge of the forest. The crowd, reluctant to leave, gradually picked up their belongings, gathered their children, waved their good-byes and trekked on home.

"She'll probably fall asleep on your shoulder. It's been a big day for her." Helena watched as William picked up little Annie, then reached for the basket.

"No doubt she's worn out; it's been a grand celebration hasn't it? And it's not over yet. There's to be a dance at the Forester's Hall and I'd like to take you, Helena."

For an instant, Helena could not respond. How could she tell this wonderful, kind man that an afternoon spent at a picnic together was one thing, but to be courted to a public dance was another. In the five years since James'death, she'd not once entertained the idea of another man. What would the children think? Then the truth struck her; Edith's strange behavior was no longer a mystery. *She must be jealous of William's attention. That's why she made the rude comments, ignored his generosity and pointed to him as she whispered to a group of girls.*

"I'm flattered, William, but to be perfectly honest, I'm accustomed to a quieter social life. Thank you for sharing a lovely afternoon, though."

William bore his disappointment gallantly. "I understand, but I hope you'll let me enjoy the company of you and your children again, Helena. I'm alone, too."

***

Since the Forester's Hall was halfway between Kelsey's General Store and the Matthews' home, Helena knew despite her fatigue, she'd get little sleep. In fact, she always felt a little nervous on the night of a dance as it was widely known that even though Prohibition closed LaBrash's Bar, bottles of home brew mystically surfaced from beneath the planks of the wooden sidewalk. Ever since Ed Forsythe had stumbled into the preacher's house at 3:a.m. last winter scaring Mrs. Malcolm out of her wits, Helena gathered her brood into her bedroom on Saturday nights. The girls slept in bed with her while the boys preferred to sleep on a mat. No, regardless of her personal reasons for declining William's invitation, she could never leave five helpless youngsters.

For the younger ones, even the resonant notes of the fiddle couldn't keep their heavy eyes from closing, but Helena noted as she brushed then braided her waist-length hair that Edith had trouble sleeping.

"Edith," her mother spoke softly. "I'd like to talk to you."

"What is it, Mama?"

"You've had something troubling you today, haven't you?"

A flaming, red mass of hair fell across the girl's face as she turned her head away in silence.

66

"It's William, isn't it?" Helena rose from her dressing table and sat on the edge of the bed. "You don't like him talking to me, do you,"

Her response was sharp. "He probably wants to marry you; stepfathers are mean and cruel. We don't need him."

"As far as I can tell," went on Helena, "William's a fine, decent man, dear. He'd make a good father for any child. But aren't you jumping to conclusions? What makes you think I'd ever remarry? I love your father as much today as when he was alive."

Relief swept over Edith's face. "You mean you wouldn't marry him, Mama?"

"I doubt if I'll ever meet a man to match your father. He was one of a kind, but I want you to understand something. There's no reason William cannot be a friend – to all of us, you included. I have faith that our Lord will watch over us as a family just as we are."

Helena smiled, placed a gentle kiss on Edith's flushed cheek and pulled the sheet over her daughter's shoulders. *How many times have I tucked you in over the years, child?* " Now go to sleep, dear. Remember, it's early church tomorrow."

Before retiring herself, Helena went downstairs, and checked to be sure the doors were secure. The chant of the 'doe-see-doe' square dance caller echoed in her ears and images of swirling skirts and high stepping lads played with her mind. She imagined dancing with William. Feeling his arms circled about her waist as they followed the other dancers. She couldn't deny she enjoyed the attention he gave her at the picnic. But should she encourage more? A respectable amount of time had passed since James's death and it was not uncommon for a widow to remarry. *Lord knows, an extra pair of hands around the house would be welcome.* Helena smiled. There was only one man who held her heart and he took it to Heaven with him.

Chapter Fourteen

"Helena, it's Josephine." The screeching hinges on the screen door announced her arrival. "Where are you? And where are the kids? It's awful quiet around here."

"I'm in the kitchen, washing the breakfast dishes my eldest was supposed to have done two hours ago. The boys are down at the creek catching frogs for bait and the girls took off with their berry buckets to pick strawberries. Cup of tea?" Soap suds disappeared as Helena wiped her hands on her apron and she reached for the kettle.

"Tea would hit the spot. I've been over at the store for the past hour stocking up on the essentials. I never knew a family could empty a flour sack as fast as ours."

"You need to stop spoilin' those brothers of yours with all your good cakes and pies. Not to mention the dozens of cookies and loaves of bread."

"You're right but they're hard working growing men and have the appetites to prove it. Oh, here I am rambling on and I have something for you. I mentioned to Mrs. Forsythe I was stoppin' by and she gave me your mail. Said it looked important."

Josephine pulled an envelope out of one of her apron pockets and handed it to her friend. Helena raised her eyebrows in curiosity as she saw the Ontario Government insignia stamped in the upper left corner. Her fingers tore open the envelope and she pulled out a sheet of paper. The letter was firm but polite.

"Dear Mrs. Matthews:

In order to keep the two-hundred acres that your late husband, James, claimed for homesteading on the Pickerel River, it is necessary that you dwell on the property. However, because of the distance from a schoolhouse, you have the option of living on the acreage for two months during the summer for the next four years or reverting the property back to the Crown. Please give the matter careful consideration. I look forward to hearing your decision. Respectfully, Dr. G. Hartford, Member of Parliament"

"Helena, is it bad news? Quick. Sit down. You've lost your color."

"I may be losing more than that." Helena's slim body slithered onto a waiting chair. "You know I told you James had intentions of building a summer home for us on the river just back of where the Forsythe's have their place.

"Yes, I remember. I've heard you speak of it often; in fact, didn't he even start on it?"

"Just the shell is standing. It's really no more than one big room with a loft but the problem is that the government intends to take it back unless we live there all summer for the next four years!"

"Lands sake! How can they do that?"

"It seems once a homesteading claim is made you must live on the actual property in order to get the deed. James wanted a place where the children could swim and fish from dawn 'til dusk. I must admit, I was looking forward to cooling my ankles in that water after a long day

70

of summer heat. I guess I never realized the government could take it away from us."

"Indian givers –that's what they are!" Josephine's face reddened. "Give with one hand and take away with the other. It's no wonder nobody trusts them. Wait 'til I tell Papa. He'll just be wild. James had a dream, Helena, don't let him down. You can beat those buzzards at their own game.In fact, I've a mind to go with you."

"Josie Bain, you can't leave the farm."

"Says who? With the size of my family helping around there, I'll never be missed. Besides, in case you haven't noticed, I have no man I'm beholdin' to; that makes me an independent woman – free to do as I choose. I want you to honor James' wishes and I know my family wouldn't think of letting you go down the river into the wilderness with five youngsters by yourself. It'll be great fun!"

"Now that I think about it, it may not be all that bad." A rosy glow replaced Helena's ashen cheeks. Forsythes go down several times a summer and Captain Walton passes twice a day with the Kawigamog. What a blessing that steamboat is for folks along the river." Her eyes sparkled with new life.

"So you'll give it a try; Helena, James would be so proud that you're willing to step out in faith. You and I know the Lord never asks more of us than we can handle. He's been with you here in the village and His presence will go with you down to the river." Josephine squeezed her friend's hand.

"Yes, I certainly am a testimony to His faithfulness. There's no disputing that. This'll be one more 'mustard seed' in our lives. I'll write Dr. Hartford this evening and tell him the Matthews family intends to homestead this summer. And Josie, finish your tea; we won't be leaving for a few more days."

71

Chapter Fifteen

"Mama, I can't wait another day!" exclaimed Billy, jumping out of his chair and almost knocking the pitcher of milk off the table. "Can't we go today; please."

Harry, catching his brother's enthusiasm echoed, "Hurry and get ready, Mama. We need to go before it gets dark so we can catch some fish."

"Whoa, boys," Helena reached out and grabbed Billy's shirt tail as he started for the door. "The river is full of fish waiting to wriggle a worm off your hooks. You'll get your chance; in fact, I'm going to depend on you two to catch many of our suppers. For now, I have things to do before we can stay away all summer. Clothes need to be packed, food prepared, cooking utensils gathered, and I'll have to ask one of the Stephens' boys to carry our things in their wagon down to the river."

"What can we do to help," volunteered Billy.

Wanting to keep the boys occupied, Helena was quick to suggest, "Round up the fishing poles your Uncle Orb made you and make sure you bring the extra hooks. You'll need the bait bucket, too, for the frogs and worms."

Within seconds the boys were planning their new adventure. Billy's head was swimming with ideas.

"We'll make a raft out of the stray logs that get away from the booms and wash up along the shore. Maybe Mr. Forsythe will give us some rope and some spikes if we tell him his kids can use it when they come down. That way we can paddle out deeper where the big pike like to hide. I sure hope our poles are strong enough to handle them. C'mon, Harry; I see him on the porch. Now let me do the talking."

A smile tickled Helena's lips. *How like his father – ready to tackle anything.*

Not all of the Matthews children were thrilled to be spending the summer alone, three miles down the river away from familiar faces.

"But Mama," protested Edith, "you promised Ruby and me that we could go over to Bain's farm this summer. It's a whole lot more fun riding on the hay wagon and feeding the chickens. We even get to help milk the cows. Who besides my silly brothers want to fish every day? I'll miss my friends and we won't be able to go to church either. I don't think God's going to be happy about that."

"Oh, is that so," returned her mother. Do you really believe the great God we believe in is so small He can only be found in the Presbyterian Church? Is his spirit not all around us? We'll be sitting in the most beautiful cathedral of all – nature; the one He made."

Edith lowered her head and she bit on her lower lip as Helena, refusing to be deterred by her daughter's hangdog look continued.

"Why, with the blue sky above, a canopy of trees sheltering us as the birds sit in the branches singing songs of praise, sunlight dancing on the water, we'll think we're already in heaven. And as far as milking the cows goes, you'll have your chance, my dear. We're taking our own cow, Bessy with us."

"But how, Mama?" inquired Ruby. "We have to row a boat across a lake to get to the river. I don't want to be in any boat with a cow!"

"Me neither, that's for sure!" chimed in Edith still eager to plead her case. "Please let us stay at the farm."

Helena was not willing to negotiate. "I need both of you to help me. Besides, Annie would be so lonesome and I don't want her wandering off into the bush. As far as Bessy goes, she'll ride on the grandest boat of all. Captain Walton will take her on his steamboat and tether her away from the water. In fact, early tomorrow morning I want you to fetch Bessy from the pasture and walk her down to the Kawigamog. The Captain and his crew will handle her from there."

"Great," sighed Edith.

"I'm sorry you're disappointed; I didn't expect to be spending our summer like this either but if we're to keep the property we have no choice. Helena put her arms around the shoulders of both her girls and gave them a hug. "We all have to pitch in and help. Who knows; you might even like it."

***

The steamboat, Kawigamog, an Indian name meaning, 'where the waters turn back', was a far cry from the canoes and rowboats used for fishing. Built for towing booms of hundreds of logs down the Pickerel River to the bush mills at Lost Channel, thirty miles away, the seventy-two foot steamer traveled about ten miles per hour. Not only was it necessary for the logging industry, but it was a lifeline for those scattered families and individuals living along the river who depended on it for delivery of goods and passengers. The 'Kwig', as it was affectionately known, had three-eighth inch steel plating from the bow back to the breast line so she could land against the

75

shoreline without damaging the wooden hull. The bow was tapered to further facilitate this method of landing for the loading and unloading of goods. Since there were few docks on the waterway, the Kwig would nudge up to the shore wherever anyone wanted to get off.

Helena knew with confidence that each time swells from the wake produced by this Grand Dame of the river splashed up against the Matthew's property, keen experienced eyes of a lean, old, weather-beaten steamboat Captain would scrutinize the shoreline for the white flag, a signal that meant she needed help.

A model of the Kawigamog

The Kwig anchored on the Pickerel River

After a day of continual activity and preparation, the children, especially the boys, were the last to give in to sleep that cast a silence over the household. The oil in the kerosene lamp burned longer than usual this evening as Helena read from a book that was as dear to her as life itself. The comforting words of Psalm 55:22, "Cast thy burden upon the Lord, and He shall sustain thee..." was all she needed to tackle what could turn out to be two months of wilderness, loneliness and any number of life's uncertainties.

Helena leaned back in her rocker and sighed. No doubt some of the men folk around the village would think she'd lost her mind. She could just hear a couple of those rough and tough lumber jacks telling their wives, "What business does a woman have haulin' those five kids three miles down the river to spend the summer livin' in a half-built cabin? She ought to give the land back to the government and let a man take it over."

But her mind was made up. This was one piece of property on the Pickerel River that would someday have a deed with the Matthews' name on it.

Chapter Sixteen

There was no time for oversleeping. With the first shaft of dawn's faint light, Helena prepared breakfast, packed last minute items into wooden crates, and coaxed five sleepy-heads from their cozy beds.

"Hurry, children; we must be ready when Sid comes to load the wagon."

"I'm ready," Billy announced as he ran into the kitchen, grabbed his cap and made for the door. He was half-way out when his mother caught him by the tail of his shirt.

"Not before you eat your porridge, son."

"Aw, Mama, I got other important things to do. Preston told me to come over to the store and get some fish hooks."

"And where do you expect to get the strength to haul in the big ones if you don't eat your breakfast?"

"Yeah, Billy," taunted his oldest sister as she came down the stairs, flinging her flaming-red pigtails over her shoulders, "if we have to eat oatmeal, you do too."

"Mama," called Ruby from the bedroom, "Annie won't get dressed. She keeps crawling back into bed."

"Billy spilled the milk," cried Harry jumping up from his chair as a white meandering stream found its way across the table and over the edge, "and it's dripping all over me!"

Amidst the confusion, Helena commanded, "Edith, help your brother. Annie I'm coming after you."

Even this fragile five-year-old knew by the hurried sound of her mother's footsteps that this was no time to play games. Off came her nightdress and it flew across the bed as she pulled and tugged a plain cotton smock over her head.

"Well, that's more like it," smiled Helena as she straightened the collar and buttoned the back. "Now, downstairs to the table with the rest of your brothers and sisters."

Finally, with all of the children seated, Helena asked a simple blessing: "Lord, thank you for the food on this table and we pray that you'll watch over us at the river this summer."

"And please let me catch a big one," added Harry. "Amen."

"Children," Helena's voice softened, "There's been a last minute change. Albert, Josephine's brother, rode down last evening to tell me their mom fell off the porch and sprained her ankle. You know she's getting feeble and was trying to reach for the clothesline and lost her footing."

Ruby gave a gasp. "Oh, Mama, that's so sad. She's such a sweet lady. Always gives us cookies when we go there. Will she be alright?"

"Should be with Josie's care."

"But Josie's coming with us. She should be here by now," announced Edith looking at the clock.

"I'm afraid we won't see our friend for a few weeks, Edith. I was looking forward to her company, too, dear. Eat up now; we have to go."

In a matter of minutes, the boys wolfed down their cereal and ran outside still chewing on bread crusts; table manners fell by the wayside this morning but Helena let it pass. " After all," she mused, "a little of their excitement has rubbed off on me, too."

Edith and Ruby were busy clearing the dishes. Annie, however, lacked any exuberance. She half-heartedly dipped her spoon into the cereal bowl and toyed with the contents.

"Annie, eat please," coaxed her mother. "We must be leaving soon."

"Not hungry."

"Are you feeling sick?" A mother's hand felt the child's face for signs of fever. Always pale, Annie's cheeks and forehead were as cool as the morning air.

"All right, Annie, off you go. We don't have time to dawdle."

For the next hour, there was constant motion as the children ran in and out of the house, supplies were loaded on Sid's wagon and Helena scurried about closing windows and locking doors. This was the first time she'd left her home for an extended stay and it seemed strange to be leaving so much behind – not just the material things but memories, too. She looked around her bedroom and her eye caught the photo of James she kept by her bedside. He'd built this home with his own hands and it was still part of him. For an instant, Helena's stomach wretched in fear and she almost shouted, "Stop! Unload the wagon. I can't handle the responsibility." But immediately calmness claimed her spirit and she resolved to finish the course James set for his family.

Checking to be sure the fire in the woodstove was out, Helena took one last look around the kitchen to be sure

81

she hadn't forgotten anything, and walked out the front door. The click of the latch told her the house was locked.

She climbed up into the wagon and turned behind to check the contents when Edith cried out, "Where's Annie, Mama? I thought she was with you."

The restless horse snorted in disgust as he felt Sid tug on the rein – like the children, the animal was anxious to move.

"Whoa, boy," Sid commanded. "That's strange. She was here while I was loading. Had to ask her to keep away from the horse. She's so tiny, you know."

"Maybe she went back into the house for something, Mama," offered Ruby.

"You might be right, dear. I've probably locked her in."

Helena ran into the house calling, "Annie, where are you?" No response. Feeling the edge of panic, she searched every room but there was no sign of Annie. *She was acting strange this morning. This is not like her.*

Helena opened her mouth to call the other children off the wagon to start combing the neighborhood when she heard whimpering from beneath the front step. There, huddled like a wounded puppy, was Annie, her eyes filled with fear.

"Annie," gasped Helena reaching for her loved one, "why are you hiding? What's wrong sweetheart?"

Between sobs and sniffles, the truth came out. "I don't want to go down the river and be eaten by a bear."

"Eaten by a bear! Whatever made you think such a thing?"

"Harry told me there are bears and if I go into the woods they'll eat me. Please, Mama, let's stay home." Annie clung to her mother's neck.

Helena wiped the dripping drops of moisture from Annie's cheeks with the edge of her shawl as she held her close. "You are not going to be eaten by any wild animal, I promise. The only thing that might bite you is a mosquito and you're plenty used to that now aren't you?"

"Yes, Mama," Annie smiled as she composed herself.

Helena's confidence waned momentarily as she realized there was some truth in Harry's insinuation. She'd been so busy preparing food and packing the family's necessities she gave no thought to the wildlife that inhabited the woods. *Lord, would you mind if I added one more thing to my prayer list?*

Sitting Annie beside her on the wagon seat, Helena turned and looked Harry straight in the eye, shook a finger at him and said, "Young man, you and I are going to have a serious talk. And I'm sure you know what it's going to be about."

Another snort from the horse and the wagon lurched forward.

Helena faced forward, put an arm around Annie's shoulder and pulled her closer.

"Sidney," she said, "This is one family the government is not going to chase off the land. We've got a right to homestead and we're on our way."

Chapter Seventeen

In half an hour, the wagon wheels skidded to a stop at the water's edge and five little bodies jumped up and spilled out in all directions. Helena gazed out over the lake; at this moment, it looked like an ocean to cross. Her rowboat was small. She wondered if it would hold six bodies and supplies, too. At this early hour, there was no one else on the lake and she knew no caring neighbors waited to help them at their destination. The nerves in her stomach fluttered like the wings of a fledgling. Was it too late to turn back? Only the coaxing voice of her eldest son put conviction back in her heart.

"C'mon, Mama," yelled Billy, "I saw a fish jump over there by the ripples. Let's go!"

That settled it; she couldn't disappoint the boys. Shaking the dust from her apron, Helena stepped over to Sid and gave him a warm hug. Indeed, he was as close to her as one of her own.

"We're going to miss you, Sidney. You've been such a help to us. I can't thank you enough. I promise I'll bake you your favorite pie when we get back."

"Ain't no bother, Mrs. Matthews." He lowered his head and pawed at the dirt with one of his boots before he continued, "You, ah, take care down there, you hear. And you kids mind your mama."

With one final burst of energy, Sid pushed the bow of the boat loaded with supplies, one mother and five children away from the shoreline and out into the deeper water while Helena maneuvered the oars until she headed the craft in the right direction. It wasn't easy; it took every ounce of strength she possessed. But for Helena, there was no other choice. Three miles of water lay between her and the homestead.

"Isn't it beautiful," said Ruby looking all around.

"Isn't what beautiful?" asked Harry.

"The lake, Harry. It's smooth as glass. And see how the sunlight makes it sparkle."

"Well, it won't be like this all day," commented Billy. "Wait 'til the wind starts blowing and the waves get so high they come splashing into the boat."

Annie started to cry. "I'm scared. I want to go home."

"It's all right, dear," Helena soothed. "Billy's exaggerating. We're going to be there in a short while."

There was, however, a ring of truth to her son's words. By noon, the water would be aroused to the point where she'd find it extremely difficult to row the heavily laden boat. Leaving before the morning mist sacrificed itself to the rising sun had lessened the burden. Each time the oars fractured the mirrored surface of the water, the skiff gained some momentum and before long the docking area became a blur in the distance.

"Mama," Edith sighed. "I'm sure going to miss Josie. I can't stop thinking about all the fun we have with her. It's not going to be the same."

"Stop your grumbling, Edith," said Billy. "That's all you've done since Mama told us we were coming down to the river."

"I have not," defended his sister. "Anyway, it's none of your business, Billy Matthews."

Before he realized what hit him, Edith reached over the side of the boat, scooped up a handful of water and threw it at her unsuspecting brother. Bedlam was ready to break out in the middle of Wilson Lake. Instantly, Helena broke the rhythm of her rowing. One hand pulled Billy's body back into his seat before he got even.

"This kind of behavior is going to get us all in trouble, you two. Do you realize how easily this boat could capsize?"

The fear in their mother's eyes was all they needed to see.

"I'm sorry, Mama," confessed Edith. "It won't happen again."

"Me too," muttered Billy glaring at his sister.

The seriousness of the moment was broken by Harry's excitement.

"Mama, keep rowing – faster, faster. I think I see a lighthouse."

"I'm sure you do, son." Helena pulled on the oars a little harder. "That's Trion's Island up ahead."

"It sure doesn't look like any house I've seen," said Annie staring intently at the white, tubular structure. "Where are the rooms? Look, the windows are all at the top."

Helena tried to explain, "I've been told that this lighthouse has only one large room at the top where the lantern is kept. The light shines through the windows at night. We'll be able to see it, too."

"You mean there's danger around this island," hastened Billy.

"Oh, there may be a few sunken logs lurking about, but this island belongs to some wealthy Americans from Pennsylvania and the lighthouse was built for fun. They use the bottom floor for dancing."

That got Edith's attention. "Bet it's not like the Forester's Hall on Saturday night, eh, Mama?"

"You're probably right, dear. I expect these folks prefer waltzes to hoe-downs."

"I imagine," dreamed Edith, "being rich and waltzing across the lighthouse ballroom in a swirling lace gown."

"Hm," sneered her eldest brother still miffed at their earlier encounter, "I'd rather be drifting across the waves fishing."

"Quiet!" demanded Harry bending his ear toward the island. "I hear voices."

"It's those men," Ruby said pointing to two moving figures. "They're waving at us. Looks like they want us to come in."

Without hesitation, Helena rowed the boat toward the island. One of the men, dressed in work clothes and carrying a hammer, met the boat.

"Morning, Ma'am. Would you by chance be Mrs. Matthews?"

"Yes, sir."

"Pleased to meet you, Ma'am. I'm Andrew; folks call me Andy." Nodding in the direction of his co-workers, he continued, "We heard you were planning on homesteading for the summer across the river. Got to hand it to you; not many would do it with such a handful." His eyes traveled from one end of the boat to the other taking in each child.

Helena's defenses went up. "I expect we'll manage just fine."

"Well, if you ever need help there's three or four of us fellers here most of the time. We're building onto the lodge if you hadn't noticed. Folks are coming up from Pittsburgh this summer, so we're working night and day to get it finished."

"I appreciate your concern," replied Helena with a softer attitude. "I don't imagine there's much we can do for you, though."

"Well, now, the boys and I were talking after we saw the Kwig unload a cow at your place. We'd be willing to pay you ten cents a quart, Ma'am, if you'd deliver milk to us."

"Harry and I could do it, Mama," Billy volunteered before Helena could respond.

Lines wrinkled her forehead as she pondered whether or not her sons were up to the responsibility.

"Look like sturdy lads to me." The worker's words dispelled some of her doubts. She'd have to trust them.

"All right. The boys will deliver the milk in the early evening."

"Horray!" The jubilant cry of the boys echoed across the water.

"Just take it up to the cook, fellows. He'll see that you get paid. Thank you, Ma'am, we'll sure appreciate it."

Helena smiled and said, "Likewise. Looks like we'll be neighbors then." With a wipe of her brow, she continued, "Take care in this temperature. I can tell already it's going to be another scorcher."

Not wishing to linger, Helena put the oars back into the water and started the last leg of the trip. By now, the day was well begun and even the smallest of God's creatures was about its business. Water bugs fascinated the children as they darted across the surface in their frenzied pattern narrowly escaping the ever present jaws of some under-water enemy.

Suddenly, everyone sat bolt upright.

"What was that?" asked Harry, his eyes bright and alert. "It sounds like a whip cracking."

89

"Nothing to be afraid of, children," Helena reassured her brood. "Look around; see if there's an animal swimming near the shore."

"Over there by that log, Mama," exclaimed Ruby. "It's a beaver."

"That's where the noise came from," explained Helena. "He smacked his wide tail against the water to warn the others that invaders are in the area. There's probably a beaver house near by."

"I see it!" squealed Annie. "It's like the one on Sturdie's Lake. Made out of branches and mud."

"Mama," cried Edith pointing to a house on a hill. "Is that our house?"

Helena turned and glanced into the foreground. There, standing desolate in a field, surrounded by woods, was their shelter for the next two months. It was small with three bedrooms and a combination living room and kitchen. Pine clap boards covered the frame and a stone chimney rose from the cedar shingled roof. She shuddered to think of what unsuspecting surprises lay hidden in each dark crevice and corner. No doubt her broom would get a good workout today.

Evening, soft as a whisper, ushered the sinking sun behind a cloudless horizon. Stars twinkled in the black velvet night while the throaty baritone bullfrogs broke the stillness. Every now and then, the lonely cry of a whip-poor-will joined in the chorus.

Inside, an exhausted Helena, sat on a plain, wooden bench with her Bible open on her lap. A faint glow from the coal-oil lamp fell across its pages but the words became a blur before her weary eyes. Like the children, who were already asleep from the activity of the day, she too needed to find her rest on the crudely constructed beds – boards covered with a straw-filled mattress.

Her lips pursed to make a breath to extinguish the lamp's flame when a gnawing sound caught her attention.

Her startled eyes pierced the dimly lit room seeking the unwanted creature. Could it be mice? She'd seen enough evidence of them while sweeping out cupboards and corners. The gnawing grew louder – too loud for a mouse. Then Helena remembered; the front steps were irregular and broken from chewing. Only one animal she knew had such a destructive habit. A porcupine. The taste of salt in lumber was an obsession with them.

There was no choice; as much as she hated to destroy a living animal, Helena knew porcupines would undermine their summer home. Picking up the axe, she cautiously opened the creaking door.

"Mama," Ruby called, "I hear a strange noise. And where are you going?"

"Shh, you'll wake the others. I need your help. Bring the lamp. We have to kill a porcupine."

"A porcupine! Mama, they're filled with long pointed quills. What if it hurts you?"

"I'll be careful. He's right beside the steps. Hold the light in front. It may blind him long enough for me to strike his head with the axe."

Trembling, but determined hands struck the animal as though it were a piece of firewood. Blood gushed out of its neck and covered the needle-sharp quills. Within seconds, the chewing stopped and the animal rolled over dead.

"You killed him, Mama. He won't chew on our steps anymore. What will we do with him?"

Helena wiped the bloody axe blade off on a clump of grass and explained, "I have to bury him so his body won't attract other animals. Thank goodness your father left a shovel in that corner near the stove. Do you think you can find it?"

"Sure. Just a minute."

In seconds she was back and handed her mother the tool, "Where should I shine the light?"

"We'll walk over to the edge of the field," instructed Helena as she lifted the porcupine onto the mouth of the shovel. "Lucky he's a small one."

Finally, with an aching back and strained eyes, Helena poured the last pile of dirt into the shallow grave and patted it down. As she walked back to the house with her daughter, Helena commented, "Even the critters are not going to keep this family from homesteading."

Chapter Eighteen

Life was simple; but life was good. Each day the children awoke to a new adventure. If they weren't swimming, they were romping through the field to investigate the near-by woods, chasing frogs or patiently sitting on a log waiting for that tug on the line. They were never disappointed; as soon as the bait sunk below the surface of the water another pickerel, bass or catfish found its way to the frying pan.

Eager to try their luck in deeper waters, the boys put together a raft, five feet wide and eight feet long, made of six cedar logs and covered with old, discarded lumber. Both boys used a long, thin board as a paddle and in true Huck Finn fashion soon became the talk of the river.

"Say, if you want to know if the fish are bit'in just ask the Matthews boys," reported the local fishermen. "They're liable to be out there on that raft rain or shine."

Even the Kawigamog came to a halt whenever the boys were sighted. Excitement rose among the passengers, especially the day Billy's crude alder pole, with the twisted wire hook, bent to the breaking point under the weight of an eight pound northern pike.

"That's a big un', Billy!" shouted the Captain. "Hang tight cause he's gonna try to break water. Give out a little more line and let him swallow the hook."

"I see him, Billy! He's huge! The biggest we've caught all summer. Don't lose him!" cried Harry.

"He's pulling me off the raft!" yelled Billy as his bare feet slid on the wet boards.

"Grab your brother around the waist and hang on to him, Harry!" advised a spectator.

"Next time he comes to the surface give the pole a good jerk backwards and you'll probably pull him up on the raft," another man coached.

By now, Billy's determination to be the victor was no match for the flailing fish. His eyes never left the swirling foamy water and with all the strength he could muster, he yanked the line out of the river landing the pike square in the middle of the raft. The fight, however, was not over yet. Desperately seeking its own environment. The fish thrashed about wildly.

"Grab him, Harry!" ordered his brother. "Don't let him jump back in."

Immediately, Harry tackled it with his body and Billy quickly thrust a wire through his gills. Cheers of triumph and applause echoed in the boys' ears as their audience showed appreciation for an unexpected show.

Later, seated on a wooden crate by the edge of the water, the Matthews family enjoyed a delicious dinner. It was simple fare-fish, caught by the boys and freshly baked bread, baked by their mother. Together, it was eaten with love.

From the left, Helena, Edith, Sue Stevens, Annie and Harry
picnic by the water while they spend the summer living
at the Pickerel River

From left: Helena, Edith, Sue Stevens, Annie and Harry

From the left, Harry and Billy show
the results of their
fishing skills - a Northern Pike

Chapter Nineteen

The outdoors was indeed the children's playground but as Helena gazed over the field where so much of their time was spent, she felt apprehensive. By the end of July, the grass was growing well over little Annie's head. Fearing the possibility that someone might step on a snake or other hidden creature, she sent word by way of Captain Walton to ask one of the farmers to come and cut the hay.

Within two days, Mr. Howes, a local farmer heeded her call for help.

"Mrs. Matthews," he called as he climbed out of his canoe, "it's Clayton Howes. I'm here to cut the field."

Helena stopped churning the milk that thickened into sweet, golden butter and ran to the door. "Come right up, Clayton. It's so kind of you to help me out."

With no effort, this burly, bearded man picked up his implements and strode up the hillside to begin his task. With lightening strokes, the razor-sharp blade of his scythe left a swath of freshly cut hay behind him. Unseen frogs and grasshoppers wisely kept one jump ahead of him.

By noon, Clayton was ready for the savory stew Helena set before him.

"Mama says you can have the hay, Mr. Howes," said Annie, "But how are you going to get it all in your canoe?"

Hearty male laughter rose to the rafters as he explained, "I won't be taking it today, Annie. First, I have to pile it all together in a stack."

"I've seen them do that down at Bain's farm," said Billy. "That's so it'll dry, isn't?"

"You're right, son. Then come winter when the river freezes over, I'll come down with my horse and sleigh and haul it back to the barn."

"I like to jump in the hayloft," commented Ruby.

"Most kids do I expect," Mr. Howes continued, "By the time I finish stacking what's out in the field, there'll be plenty to jump in."

Eager to help, the children spent the afternoon carrying armful after armful to the mounting stack. Wide at the bottom, it gradually tapered to a peak at the top. For days, the sweet herbal smell of alfalfa and grass tickled everyone's nostrils. To the boys, the haystack meant one thing – a dare.

"Bet you can't climb to the top, Harry," taunted Billy.

"Can too. Probably faster than you."

"Oh, yeah. That's what you think. Let's drag the ladder over here and we'll race."

Overhearing her brother's plans, Annie ran to join the fun.

"Get away from here, Annie," ordered Harry.

"Why? I want to jump in the haystack, too."

"Sh," Billy commanded. "Mama will hear you. Annie this is a race between Harry and me to see who can climb to the top first. You stay down here and watch. O.K.?"

Satisfied, Annie called, "One, two, three, go!"

Up the ladder and into the haystack scrambled her brothers with one little sister close on their heels. The race, however, came to a sudden halt as Helena called from the front of the house, "Harry, Billy. Come here; I need you."

Afraid of being caught, the guilty pair changed course, sliding downward on their stomachs with alarming speed. One obstacle stood in their way – Annie. There she sat, perched on the top rung of the ladder, ready to jump into the hay when, faster than she could blink an eye, the full force of Harry's weight knocked her into mid-air. Frantic, flailing arms reached in vain for the ladder. But it was too late. Fear stifled her cries. The only sound heard was that of her fragile body hitting the stubbled earth. There she lay – motionless.

"Annie, get up!" cried the boys.

There was no response.

Panic drove Harry to scream, " Mama, Annie's dead! I killed her! Hurry!"

The nerves in Helena's stomach quivered and a sick feeling stuck in her throat when she heard the fear in Harry's voice. Helena jumped off the porch, hiked up her skirt, and ran to her daughter's side. She reached for Annie's limp arm and her fingers searched for a pulse.

"Thank you , Lord," she whispered when she felt that precious throb. She examined Annie's arms and legs and assured herself there were no broken bones, but Annie had lost consciousness. Helena cast her eyes toward Harry. "What happened?"

"It's my fault, Mama," whimpered Harry and turned his face away. "I knocked her off the haystack. I didn't know Annie was sitting on the ladder, honest."

Frustrated at the children's disobedience, Helena wasn't sure if she should comfort or scold. "I know you didn't do it on purpose, but you disobeyed me, didn't you? Both of you." Her stern, parental eyes surveyed her children and demanded answers.

99

"Yes, Mama,"

"What did I tell you?"

Billy came clean. "Stay away from the haystack 'cause it's too high and dangerous."

Little rivulets of tears worked their way down Harry's dusty cheeks and spilled onto Annie's hair as he bent to kiss his sister's forehead. "I'm sorry, Annie." His broken voice whispered, "Can we pray for her, Mama?"

"Let me," coaxed Edith, her head already bent. "Please Jesus, touch our Annie like you did for the little girl in the Bible. Don't let her die; we love her and I really don't think Harry meant to hurt her. Amen."

Cradled in her mother's lap, Annie's breathing started its normal rhythm and her dazed eyes slowly opened to reveal dilated pupils. Annie lifted a hand to her head and whispered, "It hurts, Mama."

Relief dissolved the tension in Helena's body and she picked up her child with loving arms and carried her into the house. For the remainder of the summer, the haystack stood undisturbed, save the refuge it provided wet, hungry birds during the cooling rains.

Helena poses with the children by the haystack close to their summer home

Chapter Twenty

"She's coming! She's coming! I see Josephine," cried Edith from the bottom of the hill.

Like ants drawn to honey, the children scurried down to the shoreline shouting out words of welcome. The woman stepped from the canoe her brother Albert paddled, and was bombarded with hugs and kisses.

"Oh, Josie, I'm so happy to see you. It's been over a month." Helena smiled with pleasure, overjoyed to see her friend. I'd all but given up hope that you might leave the farm. How is your mama? Those sprains can be such a nuisance to mend. And did your sister have her baby? Boy or girl?" Without catching a breath, Helena turned to the man unloading a box from the canoe. "You'll stay for supper, Albert?"

"Have to get back, Helena. Appreciate the invite but evening chores have to be done, you know. Besides, it'll leave more of this fresh picked corn we brought you."

"Corn on the cob! Children, what a treat. What do you say?"

A chorus of five grateful voices responded, "Thank you. Thank you."

"Enjoy it with a feed of those fish I hear you boys are catching down here." With a twinkle in his eye, Albert pushed his straw hat to one side of his head, scratched his left ear and continued, "The talk around Forsythe's store is that you two are cleaning out the river. Got everybody worried there won't be none left for next summer."

"Aw, Albert," laughed Billy, "you're just making fun."

Harry was quick to boast, "We did catch a huge pike last week. Someone on the Kwig even took our picture."

"I'm proud of you boys. It's a big help to your mama." Albert picked up his paddle, carefully positioned himself in the canoe. "Looks like we may get a little rain; better be on my way. See you in a week, Josie. Be careful, now, you hear."

Within a matter of minutes he was a speck in the distance.

***

Churning steam rose from the hot cobs of corn Helena placed on the table. Like magnets, five hands immediately reached for a share of the bounty but quickly withdrew at the sound of their mother's chastisement.

"Children! Where are your manners? Josie will think you've forgotten everything I've taught you. And since when do we eat a meal without thanking our Heavenly Father?"

"Sorry, Mama," they uttered one by one as each head bowed in reverence.

"Thank you Father for all you've provided," Helena began, "We are especially grateful for Josephine's visit and this wonderful corn. Amen."

Finally, freshly churned butter ran like tiny rivers into the crevices of each golden kernel. Only the sounds of crunching and chewing were audible. No one refused a second helping of this tasty treat.

"Josie" asked Edith as her hunger subsided, "we thought you'd be here sooner. I looked for you every day. What happened?"

Wiping some dripping butter from her chin, Josie explained, "I wanted to come sooner, Edith, but after my mother fell and hurt her ankle, she wasn't able to walk for quite a while and I was responsible for her care and the chores around the house. Mostly the cooking. It's a big family we feed and it takes work to put three meals on the table everyday."

"I bet Albert eats a lot," Billy commented. "He's strong; I saw him lift a young calf once."

"He had to lift more than one this past month, Billy. We had something happen on the farm this summer."

"Oh?" Helena's brow furrowed. "Nothing serious, I hope."

"I'm afraid so." Josephine's eyes swept across the faces of the children and for a long moment, she was silent. When she did speak, her voice faltered and her words came slowly. "I was going to tell your mother privately," she cast a questioning look in Helena's direction and at her nod, Josephine continued, " but you children will find out when you come to the farm, so I might as well tell you now."

All chewing and rattling of utensils stopped, all eyes turned to their guest, and every ear bent toward Josephine.

"We lost our cattle."

"You mean they ran away?" interrupted Harry.

"No, Harry, Father had to shoot the entire herd."

A collective gasp went round the table.

"Even the baby calves?" Ruby asked her voice breaking.

103

"I'm sorry, but it's true. Remember in the spring three or four got sick and died. Well, the animal doctor came all the way from North Bay and examined the rest." Josephine took a deep breath. "They contacted T.B."

Helena's face turned white at the horrible news. A trembling hand flew to her face and covered lips paralyzed with fear, the same fear she had experienced years before when James had taken her to meet the Matthews.

Billy was the first to ask, "What's T.B.?"

"It's a terrible disease called tuberculosis. The animals pass it from one to the other; then they get so weak they die."

"Do people get tuberlosis?" This from Annie, barely able to pronounce the word.

For an instant, Helena saw James's sick brother and recalled that seven members of the Matthews family had died of the terrible disease. Helena regained her composure, held her tongue and simply replied, "Yes, people die of tuberculosis, too." Not wishing to dwell on the subject, Helena reminded the boys of their commitment to deliver milk to Trion's Island.

"No fishing tonight, boys."

"Aw, Mama, why not," argued Billy.

"Take a look at the sky, son. You'll be lucky to get back before it pours."

"We'll make it, Mama, don't worry," consoled Harry. "It's your turn to carry the milk, Billy. Remember?"

"Aw, shucks!" Billy grumbled on his way to the spring to haul out the gallon container. "I'm tired of delivering milk. I just wanna go fishing."

"Well, hurry up. I'll go untie the raft."

With the boys off to the island, Helena busied herself clearing the supper dishes and catching up on the local events and hear-say from Josephine. Neither women noticed how the water on the river whipped itself into a foamy frenzy. A branch from a birch tree snapped and hit the side of the house. At the same time a gust of wind slammed the front door shut and pellets of rain spat against the windows.

"Looks like we're in for a storm tonight." Josie finished wiping the last plate and looked out the kitchen window at the darkening sky. "When do the boys get back?"

"Should be soon if they did what I told them. Of course, boys will be boys and I have to tell you the lure of the river has gotten into their blood this summer. They're either on it or in it."

"I knew they'd take to it, Helena. That's one reason I encouraged you to come. Besides, what would they've done in town? Get under your feet? Or worse, pick up a few tricks from those older boys that are smokin', drinkin' and getting into all kinds of mischief. Talk is, one of those Brooks boys stole a horse from the Forshew farm and went joy riding with his girlfriend."

"I know, Josie, the older they get, the more independent they'll be and I'm bound to lose control over them. Down here I know where they are." She heaved a sigh. "At least I did an hour ago. I'm going down to the river and look for them. They'll have to row hard to keep up with this wind."

Wrapping herself in a shawl, Helena stepped outside and looked up into a caldron of dark, churning vapor. Thunder rumbled afar and raindrops spat on her face. One look at the rowboat bobbing up and down beside the shoreline confirmed her dreaded suspicions; the boys had taken their raft. With the boat, they could struggle against the white-capped waves, but with the raft, they didn't stand a chance. Anxious thoughts fed her growing concern. *Why didn't I pay more attention to the weather? All it would take is one wave to wash over the flat surface and knock them into the river. I'll just have to leave Josie with the girls, take the lantern in the rowboat and bring them home myself.*

Back in the kitchen, Helena pulled one of James's old rain slickers she'd brought from home over her head, lit her lantern, blew out the match and stuffed a handful into her apron pocket.

"Be careful, Mama." Annie threw her arms around her mother in a warm embrace.

"I won't be alone, dear. Now haven't I told you the Lord is watching over us?" Helena disentangled her daughter's arms. "Why don't you say a prayer with your sisters?"

Darkness met her as she opened the door. Pulling up her skirt, she maneuvered the front step with caution as her eyes strained in the lantern light to find the pathway to the water's edge. Lapping waves soaked her shoes as she tugged on the rope that fastened the rowboat. Finally, the knot gave way and Helena pulled the craft toward her and stepped over the gunnel and seated herself.

Helena depended on her instincts to direct her toward the island. She wasn't used to rowing into a headwind and her arms ached. Each time she stopped to rest, the wind swept her off course and she'd have to row harder. All the while, Helena called into the wind, "Billy, Harry." No response. After fifty or sixty strokes of the oars, she saw the faint glow of the lighthouse beacon. *Lord, let them be on the island. Please, let them be on the island.*

The rain, like wet, stinging pellets bounced off her bare hands as she pulled on one oar and then the other until at last her rowboat found shelter beneath the lighthouse's flickering glow. Securing the rope through a ring fastened in the dock planking, she staggered, drenched and shivering, along the pathway that led to the lodge. At first she thought it was deserted, but after three or four knocks someone opened the door.

"Mercy woman!" A robust, bald-headed little man stuck his head out. "What are you doing here on a night like this? Come in. Something wrong?"

"The boys." Each word was a gasp. "Have they been here?"

"Left about an hour ago. Storm was a'comin up fast so I told them to get on home."

"Oh, no!" Helena's weakened legs trembled and her heart beat wildly. *Help me, Lord. I need you.* "I must find them."

"Mrs. Matthews, I'd go with you but my size would be a burden trying to row in this wind. And the other men took off for town. Saturday night, you know."

"I understand. Could you relight my lantern? It's not much help but the boys might see it."

"It's the least I can do, Ma'am."

Wasting no time, the cook obliged and insisted on escorting Helena back to the boat.

"You're a brave woman, Mrs. Matthews. Don't you worry none about Billy and Harry. Both boys got good sense; they can take care of themselves. One thing for sure – you've got the wind in your favor going home. You won't be fightin' it. Goodnight, Ma'am."

The cook was right. The trip back was much easier. This time the wind pushed the boat with less effort on Helena's part. Her voice, grew hoarse from calling her sons. Guilt washed over her like a rising tide and she couldn't help thinking. *Why did I let them go? The milk could've been delivered in the morning.* These disturbing thoughts kept trying to crowd out any spec of hope, but hope refused to die. Like a voice hidden in the depths of her soul it asked her, "Where is your faith? Your mustard seed? Faith is easy to talk about -- not always easy to live but you've been down this road before and has He ever failed you? Helena's spirit surged anew.

107

The rain no longer came in sheets but lightly sprinkled her already soaked garments. Sporadic chills raced through her body and although her strength was waning, Helena called out to the blackness one last time, "Billy, Harry. It's Mama."

She waited and waited. Finally, like a heavy-hearted shepherd, Helena labored up the hill to her waiting flock.

Puddles of water followed her into the house and the warmth of the woodstove magnetically drew her to its radiating heat. Through reddened eyes, she saw everyone clustered around two shivering bodies draped in blankets. Her heart leapt at the sight of her lost sheep.

"Billy, Harry!" she flew across the room and wrapped her weary arms around both boys. "Where have you been?"

Through chattering teeth, Billy explained, "The wind blew us into the bay and we couldn't get out. It was getting dark so we left the raft and walked home."

"We delivered the milk, Mama, honest," volunteered Harry.

Tears, unrestrained, flowed down their mother's face. The cook was right; they took care of themselves. Helena reminded herself of something else. The promise of her Lord was as good tonight as it was the day He spoke to His disciples, "I will never leave you."

Thank you, Lord. Once again, You've answered my prayers. My boys have learned so much this summer.

Chapter Twenty-one

Summer was slipping away. You could feel it in the air. The evening shadows not only came earlier but they brought a nip of frost. Scattered among the evergreens, maple trees turned crimson and gold in preparation for their grand finale. The chipmunks and squirrels stuffed their cheeks with nuts and ran to their lair to deposit their winter cache. Even Bossy, the cow, changed her behavior as the children discovered one morning in late August.

"Mama," Edith shouted, running into the house with an empty milk bucket in hand. "Bossy's gone! I can't find her anywhere!"

Putting aside the broom, Helena ran to the stump where the cow was last seen tethered.

"She can't be far. We'll have to search for her. Edith and Ruby, go into the woods along the field. Annie, stay with me; and, boys take the boat and row along the shoreline. You might see her in the woods."

Within half an hour, the wandering cow was spotted. But not in the field, not deep in the woods, and not on the shoreline. Finding the terrain too rough to follow, Bossy decided to swim, with no more than her ears, eyes, and pug nose sticking out of the water.

"What will we do?" Harry asked.

"I guess we'll have to tow her home," answered his brother.

"How? We don't have any rope."

Billy thought for a moment then jumped out of his seat and made for the bow of the boat. "Sure we do. Right here. We'll use this rope."

With lightening speed, his fingers loosened the knot that held the rope to the metal ring. "You row, Harry. Lucky she's wearing a bell 'cause I'll tie the rope to her collar. Be careful with the oars. If she thinks we're going to hurt her she'll get scared and drown."

Harry was careful to maneuver the boat alongside Bossy while Billy reassured her, "It's all right, girl. We're gonna take you home."

Up came the animal's head and she gave a mournful moo.

Securing the line to her collar, Billy fastened the other end to the boat gunnel. Giving no resistance, Bossy allowed herself to be dragged through the water like a boom of logs. Every so often she'd disappear sending Billy into a state of panic, "She's going under! Row harder, harder!"

Just when the boys were convinced they'd lost her, Bossy surfaced like a whale, blowing a fountain of water from her nose and mouth. This bizarre behavior brought gales of laughter from the rest of the search party waiting on shore. Finally, the boat hit the sandy bottom and Billy unfastened the rope from the boat, jumped in the water and led the cow back to the pasture.

"Why did she leave us?" questioned Annie.

"I think she's lonesome for her old barn. It's getting cold at night," answered Edith.

"I was cold last night, too," Ruby commented. "Edith took all the covers. When are we going back to town, Mama? I miss all the kids."

Helena smiled and pulled her daughters close to her. "Soon, girls. Very soon."

Like Bossy, Helena knew their time on the river was drawing to a close – at least for this summer. They had survived and God willing, they'd homestead again until the deed to the property was theirs – fair and square.

Chapter Twenty-two

"Fire! Fire!"

The words echoed in Helena's mind until she sat straight up in bed. Shaking the grogginess from her head, she determined it must have been a dream and slid down under the blankets again.

"Fire!"

This time, she was sure; it wasn't a dream. Reality rang in her ears, each syllable magnified by the cold, paralyzing winter temperature. Grabbing her woolen robe, Helena ran into the hallway. An eerie, pink glow flooded through the front bedroom windows. She stared in disbelief as her eyes took in angry, tormented flames that engulfed Forsythe's store, that grand building full of the town's needs.

Billy awakened with a start by the increasing volume and number of gathering voices. "Mama, why are you standing there? And what's all the noise?"

One look out the window told Billy all he needed to know. His eyes widened at the galloping inferno and his excitement mounted.

"Harry, wake up! Forsythe's store is on fire! Wake up!"

Not only Harry woke, but the girls, aroused by the commotion, jumped up on the bed, huddled together, their eyes glued to the window. For the first time in their short lives, they witnessed a tragedy. Almost hysterical, Edith cried, "Grandma Forsythe. She sleeps on the top floor. She'll die, Mama!"

Helena put an arm around her shaking daughter's body and calmly said, "No dear, she's safe. I saw Ed carry his mother to the sleigh a couple minutes ago. Thank the Lord she's been spared."

"Listen to the horses," Harry's voice trembled. "They sound real strange. What's wrong with them?"

"They're frightened by all the heat and blinding light, son."

"When will the fire stop?" asked Annie. "I'm scared. Will it come here?"

No sooner were the words out of Annie's mouth when an explosion of sparks showered upward driven away by the wind. Helena shuddered. She knew that any one of the sparks could put their house in danger.

Suddenly, the whole scene changed as the intense heat, not fifty yards away from Helena's home, met the extreme cold on the window panes and splintered glass in all directions. The children screamed and reached for their mother.

"It's all right," she reassured, her voice quivering, "we'll stay away from the windows. Come downstairs and we'll sit in the parlor."

"I heard a knock," said Harry. "Listen."

"Someone must need help." Helena raced ahead of the children to unlock the front door. Before her stood Matt Stephens and the 'Dummy', smelling of smoke, their faces strained and smudged with soot.

"Helena, I wanted you to know that Anthony and me are keeping a watch on your house, so don't let them sparks frighten you."

Helena let out a sigh of relief. "Thank you, Matt; that's been a worry. I don't know how many windows I've lost from the heat. Sure you've lost some, too."

"Glass can be replaced. Let's pray that's all we lose."

"Of course, you're right."

Shouts of warning put an end to their conversation. "Move back, move back! She's fallin' in!"

Instantly, their heads turned toward the inferno. Like a giant oak tree, cut and ready to fell, down came the top balcony sending up another cascade of roaring flame. Next the roof collapsed. Anthony's eyes grew moist as he watched the hours of labor he lovingly put into carving the beautiful façade brutally destroyed.

Helena's heart went out to her friend who would never be able to put his sorrow into words. Gently, she touched his arm and he turned so he could read read her lips.

"We'll never forget, Anthony; the skill and beauty you put into the store will be talked about for years."

A weak smile crossed his face.

"I feel so helpless. It's such a waste."

"Helena, a pot of coffee would sure feel good to most of us fellers. We've been fightin' a losing battle but we're gonna have to see it through to the end."

"Certainly, Matt. I'll have it ready in no time. Please send the men over." Helena paused. "I'm afraid to ask, but have there been any casualties?"

"Polly."

Helena gasped. "Oh, no. The children are going to take this hard."

"Not just the children. Everyone loved Polly. Why, that parrot could talk like she was human. I reckon there wasn't time for Ed to go back in for her. Thank God he was able to carry his mother down all those steps."

"You're right. Things are bad enough but the family is safe."

It was close to dawn when Helena stood on her front porch and watched the defeated, weary townsfolk trudge back home for a few hours sleep. The nightmare was still vivid. All that was left of Forsythe's General Store was a few smoldering beams. And memories. Who could forget the pungent odors of leather, wax, oats, molasses, peppermint and licorice? Who in the village had not stepped through her doors and shared in the good-natured fun of championship checker and card games, laughter, tears, or children's tom-foolery? How many folks, weary after a long day's toil, took rest in the rockers lining the front porch?

With one last lingering look, Helena sighed, went inside and closed the door.

Chapter Twenty-three

"Uncle's coming! Uncle's coming!" Annie bounded up the steps throwing open the front door. Newborn snowflakes fell from her woolen coat like hairs from a shedding dog.

"Annie Matthews," scolded Edith, "I've mopped this hallway. Out you go."

"But Uncle Orb is here. Can't you hear him?"

Sure enough, the shiny brass sleigh bells attached to the horse's harness jingled with each prance of laboring hooves.

"How do you know it's Uncle Orb?"

"Because his sleigh bells sound the best. Anyway, it has to be him. I'm all ready to go to Grandma's."

"Well, hold your horses, young lady. You know he always brings Mama a load of firewood and we have to help unload it."

"Then hurry up and get your coat and mittens on. Look, here he is."

As expected, Helena's brother Orb Campbell, a short man of vim and vigor, jumped down from the sleigh and gathered Annie up in his arms. Every year since

James's death, two days before the birth of the Christ Child, he delivered a load of wood to Helena, packed the family into the sleigh and returned to the Campbell homestead in Restoule. Being a widow for several years, Helena appreciated any help her family was able to give.

"When can we go, Uncle? Did Grandpa pick out a Christmas tree yet? Has Grandma baked any gingerbread cookies?"

"Whoa, little one. First things first and that means your ole uncle could stand a cup of your Mama's hot tea. It's cold out on that trail."

"We'll do better than that, brother," announced Helena from the doorway. "Got some steaming vegetable soup and fresh buns."

"I don't want to eat; I just want to go to Grandma's house," pouted Annie.

"Christmas isn't going to come any faster, dear. Go round up your brothers. It's time for lunch."

By two o'clock, the wood was stacked in rows and the winter sun was on its decline. Orb knew that as the daylight dropped below the horizon, the temperature soon followed.

"Wrap the newspapers tight around those hardwood blocks, boys." instructed their uncle. "We've a long trip ahead of us."

"Mama has put a lot of things in the oven, Uncle Orb, but she sure doesn't bake too many blocks of wood," commented Billy.

"It's an old trick, son. But it works. Keeps your feet from freezing. Is everyone ready?"

"Yes, yes," chanted the girls as they huddled beside their mother in the back of the sleigh. A heavy woolen blanket tucked around their legs trapped the warmth of the wooden heater. The boys preferred to sit up front with their uncle, patiently waiting for the moment he'd hand the reins over and tell them it was their turn to command the horse.

To Helena, this sleigh ride was a highlight. For the next few hours, she had the opportunity to quietly appreciate her surroundings. Gliding past farm yards that bordered the Spring Creek road, they waved and shouted, "Merry Christmas!" to young and old. Occasionally, they'd pass another team of snorting horses pulling a cutter to town. The open fields lay like sheets of purest white linen, covering the resting earth below. Eventually, the scene changed; no more were they subject to the wind sweeping across wide open spaces, but now they were sheltered by the deepening forest. Hemlock, oak, and pine trees stood like sentinels.

Helena inhaled the tingling, fresh scent of thick evergreens as they spread their snow-laden branches in all directions keeping out the north wind's bite. Rabbits hopped about leaving miniature snow-shoe tracks wherever they went.

"Look, Mama!" Ruby sat up and pointed to a doe. Startled by the sleigh bells, it pivoted through the air as gracefully as any ballerina, then disappeared into the thicket. "It's my favorite animal. But where's its mother? I hope a hunter didn't shoot it."

A breath of white frost proceeded Helena's comment. "I hope not, dear, but you know sometimes we depend on animals God meant us to eat."

"I know. I try not to think of the deer when grandpa brings us our venison." Ruby closed her eyes and snuggled closer to her mother.

Anticipation among the children grew as the sleigh broke into an open field. They saw the petrified smoke rise from their grandparent's chimney straight into the frigid twilight sky.

"We're here, Annie," shouted Orb. "Your grandma will soon hear the bells and I'll bet you a dollar to a doughnut she's waiting at the door for you."

119

In no time, the thick oak door of the homestead opened and Grandma Campbell stood with arms extended, ready to wrap them around the first grandchild out of the sleigh. There was no way any of them could wrestle out of her embrace – nor did they want too. Especially, Annie who clung to her neck, hugging her grandmother over and over.

"Grandma, where's Snowball?" Annie snuggled closer. "She's always here at the door to meet us."

A short silence followed before Grandma Campbell answered, "Annie, Snowball has disappeared. It's been a week since I last saw her."

The words hit Annie as hard as any physical blow. The excitement and glow in her face turned to pale disbelief.

"But Grandma, she's my favorite cat. I love to feel her soft fur and you remember how she purrs in my ear."

"I know, dear; I miss her, too."

It was a sad little girl who pushed the meat and potatoes around her supper plate. Helena, sensing her daughter's grief, did not fuss at her to finish her meal. The hurt was real. Nor had it lessened by bedtime.

"Mama," Annie whispered as Helena tucked her under a quilt, "close your eyes and pray with me."

"Of course, dear. You want to talk to God about Snowball, don't you?"

"Yes, because you've always told me that He watches over us. Right?"

Helena nodded in agreement as she laced her fingers together with Annie's and her childish voice offered the prayer, "Please keep Snowball warm and safe tonight and it would sure make me happy if You brought her back to Grandma. Amen."

Chapter Twenty-four

A heavy, dark cloud hung low over the horizon the next morning causing Grandpa Campbell to suggest, "After breakfast, we'd be wise to get on over to the woods and cut our tree. If it snows hard, we won't be able to find the kind your Grandma likes, kids. And you know how particular she is about her Christmas tree." He gave his wife a teasing smile. "Who's coming with me?"

A chorus of "Me. Me, too. I will, Grandpa," echoed around the table.

"I didn't hear you, Annie. Aren't you going to help your Grandpa get the tree this year?"

"Can we look for Snowball on the way?"

"Sure we can but you know she might be hard to see in the snow with all her white fur."

"I know, Grandpa, but we have to try. I'm sure she's out there somewhere."

The sleigh that went out to the woods came back with its cargo of snow-covered children, one tired grandfather, and the bushiest sweet-smelling spruce in the forest. But no Snowball.

As the day wore on, Annie's Christmas spirit dropped like the chilling outside temperature.

"Annie, can I eat your ginger cookies?" begged Harry. "You left two on your plate and one has a bite gone. Don't you like them?"

"Not hungry."

"Well, come help string popcorn for the tree and then Mama says we can go outside to play Fox and Goose in the snow. You love that game. We'll even let you be the fox," shared Ruby.

"Grandma," Annie whispered, "Christmas without Snowball just isn't going to be the same this year."

The excitement and anticipation of celebrating Christ's birth grew each day as Grandma Campbell checked off another completed task: cookies, pies and cakes baked, floors and windows scrubbed, gifts wrapped, tree trimmed and evergreen boughs hung over the mantel. One last minute chore remained and this was Grandpa Campbell's responsibility. Early, the day before Christmas, before the children awoke, he sharpened the blade of his axe and sought the fattened turkey. Sometime before lunch, a twenty-five pound gobbler sat in the waiting roast pan.

"Let me help, Grandma," Annie begged as she grabbed a fistful of savory sage bread dressing and rammed it into the bird's empty cavity.

"Make sure you don't lose any, sweetheart. I have to admit, folks always come back for second helpings of my dressing."

Annie managed a weak smile. "I even like it before the turkey cooks it. Raw onions are good. See." She popped a chunk into her mouth and chewed until tears ran down her cheeks.

"Mercy, child! Now go ask your mother to give you the string and my darning needle so I can sew up this hole before you eat every crumb."

122

Annie was half-way off the stool when the door opened and a blast of cold air swept through the kitchen.

"They're coming! They're coming!" Harry's voice grew louder as he bounced across the threshold, snow falling from his woolen coat and hat. "Listen. You can hear the bells."

In a matter of moments, three cutters glided up to the rail fence that protruded through the mounting snowbanks. Aunts, uncles, cousins and friends disembarked, each clutching a package or some favorite delicacy and marched up to the front door shouting, "Merry Christmas!"

Hugs and kisses smothered rosy cheeks as the spirit of love circulated from one to another. After the initial commotion died down, Grandma invited everyone to the huge oak table where bowls of steaming potato soup and crispy, golden biscuits waited to satisfy the heartiest appetite.

All afternoon, the children busied themselves playing outside. The men gathered in the barn to finish the chores and the women caught up on the latest local news while sipping tea from Grandma's special bone china cups. After supper, as twilight turned to darkness, Grandpa Campbell got down the well-worn family Bible, settled himself in the rocker beside the fireplace, and turned to Luke, chapter two. A hush came over the children as they recognized this as a signal to gather round their grandfather's feet and give him their undivided attention. A soft glow from the small flickering candles on the tree fell across each page illuminating the sacred words as once again Grandpa's baritone brogue brought the Christmas story alive. He barely finished when a cousin's crystal-clear soprano voice began to sing Silent Night, Holy Night. One by one others joined in except for one heartbroken little girl who crept upstairs unnoticed and buried her face in her pillow.

Chapter Twenty-five

"Annie, wake up!" Harry shook his sister until she tossed the quilt at him. "Come downstairs; hurry!" With one hand he tugged her out of bed and dragged her down each step.

"I don't care what's in my stocking."

"It's not in your stocking, and there's more than one. Look under the tree."

Annie's face beamed. Beneath the branches sat Snowball, a brand new mama cat, licking three of her five babies. The other two, with eyes barely open, were pawing at the needles on the bottom branches.

"Mama, Grandma, Grandpa, Snowball's back!" Annie's enthusiasm was a wake-up call for everyone. Within minutes, the whole family gathered around the tree to share Annie's joy.

"Our prayer was answered, Mama." Her blue eyes sparkled with gratitude as she lifted them to her mother's face.

"His timing is always perfect, little one. Remember that."

"Well, now we know why she disappeared, don't we," offered Grandpa.

"But where did she go?"

Grandpa chuckled. "She found a warm spot back in the storage room. After I was pretty sure everyone had gone to bed last night, I went in there to get your Grandmother's gift. I have to hide it, you know, cause I think she peeks." An affectionate wink passed between husband and wife. "While I was in there, I heard the babies. I almost ran upstairs to tell you, Annie, but you were asleep and I knew your mama would have a fit if I woke you." Helena smiled at her father in agreement as he continued, "So, I did the next best thing and put them under the tree for the rest of the night."

"Oh, thank you, Grandpa." Annie locked her arms around his neck. "I'm so happy. It's the best Christmas ever!"

Chapter Twenty-six

Seasons came and seasons went. For the first five years after James's death, time in Helena's mind, moved slowly. The dauntless task of caring for a home and five children on her own often brought her to her knees. But as the children grew and her prayers became answered blessings, time took on another dimension. It flowed forward like a river eager to meet the ocean. *If only I could reach out and slow life down. Lord, my children are growing more independent. Each day they need me less. I've held them so close to me; please give me the courage and the wisdom to know when it's time to open my arms and let them go.*

Conversations with God were commonplace for Helena, especially when she worked in her garden. Hoeing all morning in soil full of lumps of clay was a task Helena did not enjoy, especially, since the hoe bounced off a piece of hardened earth, struck her foot and left a nasty gash. Lifting her foot from the blood-stained water basin, she was halfway through wrapping strips of an old pillowcase around the injury when the screeching hinges on the screen door caught her attention. She turned her weary body in time to see Edith, her hair braided in a new style and perched like a crown on top of her head, walk in with the mail. One look at her mother's misfortune and she gasped.

"What happened, Mama? Are you all right?"

"Yes, dear, don't fret. I'm fine. My foot will mend, but," Helena sighed long and hard, "the shoe won't. The hoe slipped and went right through the leather."

"Let me fix you a cup of tea, Mama. That always perks you up. Oh, I almost forgot; here's a letter for you. It's postmarked Haileybury. Must be from Uncle Yacht."

"Let me see. Yes, that's his handwriting." Helena tore open the envelope and unfolded the stationary. A fifty dollar bill slid onto her lap. "Well, now what's this?" Helena read the letter and she completely forgot about her injury. "Edith, forget the tea. Come here and listen to this."

Puzzled, but anxious, she came and sat by her mother.

"Do you still want to become a teacher?"

"More than anything, Mama. You know that. I can't read enough books and Mrs. Malcolm says I'm doing a fine job teaching the primary class at church. But I need more schooling and you don't have the money to send me anywhere."

A smile erased any physical discomfort Helena felt earlier. "I do now." She held up the fifty dollar bill. "Listen to your uncle's letter."

Edith was all ears.

Dear Helena,

Please consider the suggestion I have to offer. Now that Edith is sixteen and ready to further her education, Maude and I would like to have her come to Haileybury. There is a fine school here called Monteith Academy. It is a government school, therefore no fee is required to attend. The enclosed money, however, would help with clothing and transportation. Edith is a fine, young lady and deserves to pursue a profession. Give it some serious thought and let me know what you both decide. Lovingly,Yacht

"Oh, Mama. I can't believe it! You'll let me go, won't you?" Edith's eyes danced with excitement.

Helena took her daughter's hand, no longer a child's but a maturing young woman's. "I want every opportunity for my children, dear. You'll make a fine teacher; do your father proud." A warm embrace between the two put any doubts Edith had to rest. "Now, how 'bout that tea?"

Top row, left to right:
Harry, Helena, Edith, friend

Bottom row, left to right:
Ruby, Edward Simms
(Edith's beau)
Annie

129

Chapter Twenty-seven

"Save a piece of cake for Billy and me, Ruby." Harry ran his finger around the rim of the mixing bowl scooping up a mouthful of pink icing. "Probably be close to dark when we get home. Mr. Clapperton says chore boys have to check all the tourists' boats in the evening 'cause they might have fish to be cleaned."

"That's part of your job isn't it?" Ruby smacked her brother's fingers as he went for seconds.

"Yeah, I know, but it seems all we do is clean fish; we never get a chance to catch them anymore. At least not like when we were living down the river. I wish we were still spending our summers there."

"Well, I'm happy Mama finally got the deed to the property. It was lonely for her being away from her friends and you know how she missed Sunday church. Anyway, I heard her tell Mrs. Forsythe yesterday that when they go down to their place in August, we might go for a week or so."

Harry let out a yell of delight.

"Sh, Annie's still asleep. You'll wake her up and this birthday cake is supposed to be a surprise."

"All right, but don't forget to save some for her hard-working brothers." Picking up his lunch pail, Harry left the kitchen licking his lips. "Birthday cake is one of my favorites."

For the children, July 20, 1923, was a day to celebrate Annie's tenth birthday. For Helena, this date was both sweet and sour for it was a cruel reminder of James's death.

Helena stopped shelling the peas that lay in her apron and rested her head on the back of the rocker, her mind traveling backward over the years. She couldn't believe it had been ten years since his burial. So much had happened. The world went to war, gas driven wagons were no longer a novelty, Prohibition was the law of the land, and some women in the cities were wearing dresses hemmed at the knee.

The melancholy she felt this time of year weighed heavier than usual and that afternoon she confessed to Josephine, "I don't know, maybe I feel this way because of the changes going on in the children's lives. They don't need me as much. The older ones are starting to find their own way in the world. Come September, Edith will be gone to school two or three hundred miles away. Why, according to Annie, she even has a beau."

Josie's eyebrows lifted in curiosity. "Who is he? And how does Annie know?"

"Saw Edward Simms walk her home from church," Helena smiled, "and of course Miss Prying Eyes tells me they were holding hands."

"Edward's a good fellow; no need to worry. Besides, they'll find out if absence makes the heart grow fonder once she leaves for Haileybury, won't they?"

"Good point."

"Then," Helena took a sip of tea, "next year Ruby will be ready to leave. She's already talking about learning secretarial skills. She'll have to go to the city to get trained

132

and find a job. If I've learned one thing these past ten years, Josie, it's that I want my girls to be prepared for the future. God forbid they end up with a fate like mine; life is so uncertain."

"Women are doing things we never dreamed of when we were young, Helena. How exciting it is for them. What do you see for the boys?"

"They're country boys. I can't see them finding contentment in the city. If they can't pick up a pole and head for the river when they fancy, they'll be a fish out of water. Who knows, the way this part of the country is opening up to the tourist trade, maybe they'll have a business of their own."

Josie leaned across the table and squeezed her friend's hand. "Be proud of them; I know it's been hard but I'm thinking the worst is over. You've shown them the way. Taught them right from wrong. What more can a mother do?" Josie's voice became wistful, "Course never having had children of my own, what do I know?"

It was Helena's turn to comfort, "You may not have bore any but many a child in this village has felt your love—your encouragement. In fact, last week after Annie spent the day with you, she told me, "Mama, Josie let me knead the bread. I punched and punched the dough to make it rise. She said it was the best bread she'd ever eaten."

"She's a sweetheart," said Josie looking at her pendant watch then jumping up from the table with a start. "Lands! I need to get home. I promised my mother I'd wash her hair today."

After hugging her friend good-bye, Helena, wearily climbed the stairs to her room anxious to take a nap before Annie's celebration began. There was no better teacher than experience and Helena knew a houseful of energetic children, both hers and the neighbors', would tax her to the limit.

133

Meanwhile, downstairs, the party celebrations began in earnest with Edith giving the orders.

"Hurry, Ruby, get out the best tablecloth and napkins. Annie, run over to Mrs. Stephens and tell her she can start making the ice-cream."

Annie's face shone with happiness. "It's going to be the best surprise, isn't it? I can't wait for all her friends and family to get here."

"Stop standing around, sister, they're coming in an hour. And don't slam the door; you'll wake up Mama."

By five minutes to four, the floors were swept, the furniture dusted and the table set, complete with a centerpiece of daisies, buttercups, and black-eyed susans. Outside, sounds of a naying horse and the creaking of wagon wheels caught the girls' attention.

"They're here! Grandma and Grandpa are here." Annie bolted out the door and ran into her grandmother's waiting arms.

Annie could barely contain herself. "Grandma, Mama thinks you're here for my party. She doesn't know lots of people are coming too. Look, there's the Simms's and down the road I see the Forshew family. C'mon with me Grandma. Let's go wake her up."

Awakened by the talking and laughter outside, Helena rose and peeked out the window. *Heavens! Why are all these folks coming to my house?* She quickly straightened her skirt, took a look in her mirror while she pinned back a stray strand of graying hair.

She thought it strange no one was coming in and when she got to the last step on the stairway Annie swung the front door open, grabbed her hand and pulled her outside.

"Surprise!" a cheer went up from the crowd.

Helena's eyes widened and she shook her head trying to explain, "No, no. It's Annie's birthday. She's ten today."

134

Grandma Campbell stepped forward and hugged her daughter. "We know, dear, but this year is special and Annie is sharing her celebration."

Reverend Malcolm removed his hat and explained to Helena, "We townsfolk know that today brings back memories of not only Annie's birth but James' passing. You never were able to give his burial a proper closing and you deserve nothing less, Helena. Although this may be unusual, your friends and family are here today, ten years later, to help you do that. Come, sit up on the wagon. We're going for a short ride."

By the time the entourage assembled at the cemetery where James lay in rest, Helena's pulse beat normally and her breathing no longer came in short pants. Even now she wasn't quite sure what to expect. Her eyes followed their familiar pathway to the tall, black and gray marble and granite headstone standing proudly at the head of a grassy mound. She'd visited so often she knew the epitaph by heart. *"Death is certain; the hour unseen."*

Gathering around the gravesite, Reverend Malcolm spoke this prayer, "Father in Heaven, as friends and family of John James Matthews, we gather today to celebrate his life. To give his wife, Helena, and his five children, Edith, Ruby, Billy, Harry and Annie an opportunity to publicly express their love and reflect on the wonderful husband and father he was to them.

A soft murmur of agreement rippled among the crowd and more than one spotless, white handkerchief wiped away a sniffle or tear.

The reverend continued, "Yes, we are sad because we miss our brother. He was a man of exceptional vision; but, I believe his courage left us all a little stronger. A little more determined to step out and be everything God intended us to be. And the last gift he gave us we celebrate today; his little Annie. Although his eyes never gazed on her, our eyes see her father in her. Let us be thankful for her gift of life. Amen."

Reverend Malcolm turned to a lady holding a beautiful wreath of freshly cut flowers, nodded to her and simply announced, "Mrs. Simms."

She handed it to Helena and said, "Each of us has taken a bouquet from our gardens and entwined them into a circle. This circle represents the unbroken love we felt for James and for you and the children."

Helena's cheeks were wet from tears; tears of sadness and tears of gratitude to all who demonstrated their love to her family today. After giving Mrs. Simms a hug, she responded, her voice shaking, "What a wonderful lesson you've all taught my children today. They've seen the spirit of our Lord at work and I pray that what they've witnessed, they will pass on in their lives. Thank you all for coming and Reverend I appreciate your kind words." Helena took a deep breath and with a smile on her face announced, "Now, since this is a day of celebration, I happen to know birthday cake is being served at the Matthews's home and you are all invited."

"Ice-cream, too," shouted Annie, eager to start her party.

While the townsfolk turned and retreated, Helena stepped toward the grave, placed the flowered wreath beneath the headstone and whispered, "I love you, James."

-The end-

A monument stands in memory of John James Matthews
in the village cemetery

Epilogue

Helena Matthews passed away January 30, 1951, at the age of seventy-four. Her body simply wore out after many years of toil. She never remarried but found joy and contentment in her family. Each of the children grew into responsible adults who honored their mother by exhibiting the core values she taught them throughout their lives.

Edith became a teacher and taught two years before she married Edward Simms, August 19, 1929. They ran a successful tourist and fishing business at Edward's Island Inn at Port Loring on Wilson Lake. They had three children- Lois, Anne and Ted.

Ruby became a stenographer and married Ivan Donnelly, October 17, 1930. They operated a garage and filling station for several years in Loring. They had three children- Lawrence, Adele and Diane.

Billy married Pearl Forshew, September 9, 1939. They built and operated a fishing lodge on Memesagamesing Lake. They had four children – Gael, Johnny, CarolAnne and David. Bill died of a heart attack at age forty-nine while working his trap-line.

Harry married Jennie Brooks, January1, 1938. They operated a fishing and hunting lodge, Pine Lake Camp, for over thirty years. They had three children- Jimmy, Patsy(deceased at age ten months) and Sally.

Annie became a teacher and taught two years when she contacted tuberculosis and spent a year in the Gravenhurst Sanitarium where she died at age twenty-one, October 1, 1936.

18723542R00084

Made in the USA
Charleston, SC
17 April 2013